SIGNS

AND

WONDERS

THE UFO DECEPTION

CHUCK NELSON

SIGNS
AND
WONDERS
THE UFO DECEPTION

In later times some will depart from the faith by devoting themselves to deceitful
spirits and teachings of demons.
[1 Timothy 4:1]

RELIANT
PUBLISHING
A DIVISION OF REDEMPTION PRESS

Published by Reliant Publishing, an imprint of Redemption Press, PO Box 427, Enumclaw, WA 98022.
Toll-Free (844) 2REDEEM (273-3336)

Reliant Publishing is honored to present this title in partnership with the author. The views expressed or implied in this work are those of the author. Reliant Publishing provides our imprint seal representing design excellence, creative content, and high-quality production.

ISBN 13: 978-1-64645-686-4 (Paperback)
978-1-64645-688-8 (ePub)
978-1-64645-687-1 (Mobi)

Library of Congress Catalog Card Number: 2022905198

Contents

Introduction

Almost everyone has seen the fascinating videos of UFOs recorded by our military in recent years. We have been seeing these videos on the nightly news rather than on sensational or science-fiction programs where we normally might expect to see them. If you have been paying attention, you know that the military has admitted that these are real videos of Unidentified Flying Objects encountered by military aviators and other personnel, and they are routinely tracked and recorded by various military sensing technologies. While the military has traditionally denied and downplayed UFO reports, it turns out that various branches of the military have been spending millions of dollars investigating UFOs for many years. In a recent public document, the Department of Defense has admitted that UFOs are real, but they don't know what they are.

If you mention the term UFO or flying saucer in a group of people, you are bound to see some rolled eyes or at least some raised eyebrows. Most people don't give a lot of thought to UFOs or flying saucers and tend to relegate them to science fiction, excessive imaginations, or fraudulent stories. For the most part, this is a reasonable way to approach UFO stories. When UFO sightings are investigated by qualified personnel, most turn out to be misidentified natural phenomena, conventional aircraft, or fraudulent reports. Accordingly, it is reasonable to approach reports of UFOs and extraterrestrial beings with caution.

However, when fraudulent reports and natural phenomena are excluded, there remains a percentage of UFO reports that are unexplainable by modern science and technology. These unexplainable reports often involve credible witnesses and confirming physical evidence in forms such as photographs, videos, radar confirmation, or confirmation by various military target-tracking technology. Something real is happening, and it cannot be said that all UFOs are figments of someone's imagination or entirely natural phenomena. Military and civilian technology have tracked UFOs performing maneuvers that defy known physics and human technology. Even the United States government now states that UFOs are real, physical objects, often operating in restricted airspace. It turns out that UFOs or similarly depicted aerial phenomena have been described throughout human history. The question that confronts us is not just "What are they?" We must also ask, "Who is behind the UFO phenomenon?"

Given the indisputable reality of some UFO phenomena, every thinking person will have to decide what to do with this information. Every individual giving thought to the UFO phenomenon must, at some point, consider the "what" and "who" issues. This includes Bible-believing Christians. How should Christians address these signs and wonders in our skies? In my experience, most Christians seem content to ignore the UFO phenomenon because they don't know what to do with it. Some may find the idea that UFOs are real to be threatening to their worldview or theology. Others are just uncomfortable with the social stigma attached to UFOs or find them too incredible to consider. UFOs, as such, aren't mentioned in the Bible, but we will see that the Bible does give us the information we need to identify the "what" and "who" questions that arise in relation to the phenomenon.

UFOs are an unconventional phenomenon that defies conventional explanation. Without a conventional explanation to reference, many are reluctant to express—or even consider—an unconventional explanation. UFOs defy our sense of reality, and "normal" people don't usually talk about them. At least, that has been the case in the past. Still, today, many find it expedient to avoid or ignore the UFO phenomenon rather than try to explain it or fit it into their worldview. Unconventional explanations are uncomfortable to consider, and openly expressing one can attract ridicule. The undeniable reality of UFOs has massive theological and scientific worldview implications for anybody. Ignoring the issue doesn't make the phenomena go away. UFOs persist in appearing in our skies and news reports, so it is imperative for Christians to take the time and make the effort to see how the UFO phenomenon fits into the Christian worldview.

The culture at large is seeing increasingly hard evidence of UFO activity from civil and military sources. The traditional denial of the existence of UFOs by the government has been replaced by affirmation and reliable evidence of their existence. In June 2021, the United States Department of Defense published an official document acknowledging the physical reality of Unidentified Aerial Phenomena or UAPs, which is their preferred term for UFOs.

Along with everybody else, Christians can no longer credibly deny the reality of UFOs. A 2021 survey by CBS News determined that two-thirds of the United States population believe in extraterrestrial alien intelligence.[1] The UFO phenomenon is much more than an issue of science and technology; it has deep theological and worldview implications. The culture is deciding the "what" and "who" of the UFO question from a secular perspective. Christian leaders and the church need to be prepared to address the reality of UFOs from the context of a biblical worldview. Millions of people worldwide believe they have been contacted by alien entities associated with UFOs and are learning their theology. This sounds unreal or even bizarre to consider. UFOs are already unreal and bizarre . . . yet real. Are millions of people irrational, or are they being deceived? Will the church be silent, or does it have a biblical perspective and relevant message for the culture in the face of the UFO phenomenon?

In this work I realize I am running the risk of being identified with Chicken Little, who claimed, "The sky is falling." Be assured, I am not claiming the sky is falling or doom is on the horizon, but I believe I am identifying a legitimate concern for the secular public and especially for Christians and particularly Christian leaders. I admit that it is something of a struggle to address an incredible subject matter in a credible way. I am willing to risk my personal credibility because the UFO phenomenon has significant social and theological implications that exceed the interests and domain of secular science.

In this work I will attempt to address the "what" and "who" of UFOs from the perspective of a biblical worldview. My objective is to inform and encourage interested parties, including Christians and especially Christian leaders, to confront and examine the UFO and related phenomenon from a biblical perspective. The UFO phenomenon is not going away and will continue to attract attention as worldwide interest grows and our government gears up for a more intense study of it.

As part of the UFO phenomenon, I will be discussing the even more controversial subject of alien encounters and abductions. Until I looked into the matter, I thought alien-abduction reports were limited to a small number of disingenuous or mentally disturbed individuals. Upon investigation I found it's a worldwide phenomenon involving millions of people, most of whom have no history of mental dysfunction. These reported abduction experiences contain certain commonalities that are interesting but disturbing. Many people are deeply troubled by what they perceive to be alien-abduction experiences. Most pastors are ill-equipped to address the issue let alone help these people, so the experiencers frequently seek help from groups formed by others who have had similar experiences. Within these groups, the abduction experience is reinforced and accompanied by theological views leading far from a biblical worldview.

This is a short and shallow presentation of this subject matter, but it is intended to challenge others to a more thorough study of the subject. By extension, this work is also a warning for Christians and especially Christian leaders not to ignore the UFO and alien-encounter phenomena. The implications are paradigm-shattering and worldview-changing. This book is about much more than UFOs in the sky. It's about worldviews and the nature of reality. Yes, it can be bizarre, but get over it— it's real, and it's happening.

For readers interested in greater detail on this subject matter, I recommend the following books for starters:

Books with a Christian-Biblical Perspective

Alien Intrusion[2] This is a contemporary and comprehensive book and resource. I highly recommend it.

Alien Encounters[3] This book is not as contemporary as *Alien Intrusion*, but comprehensive, presenting a perspective that serious Christians need to consider.

Books with a Secular Perspective

(Recommended for mature Christians with a sound biblical worldview)

Abduction: Human Encounters with Aliens,[4] *Abduction* was written by a Harvard psychiatrist who has interviewed and treated many individuals who claim to have been abducted by aliens. In the course of this book, the reader becomes familiar with the abduction phenomenon and the theology expounded by entities perceived to be UFO-associated aliens. The contrast between ET's theology and a biblical worldview is evident, but importantly, the impact of ET's theology on the secular mind is equally apparent. It is interesting to note that the author, like so many alien-abduction researchers, appears to invest to some measure in the reality of the abduction accounts as well as the theology of the aliens.

Skinwalkers at the Pentagon: An Insiders' Account of the Secret Government UFO Program[5] This book is an insider look at a recently concluded twenty-two-million-dollar government research project into UFOs and related paranormal phenomena. Don't let the title throw you off; this book is important in that it documents incredible and physically hazardous encounters with UFOs and associated paranormal experiences. It's the scariest book I've read in years. While the events recorded are incredible, the scientists and researchers collecting, researching, witnessing, and recording the events are exceptionally credible. However, this book is written from a secular perspective and lacks the biblical insight to recognize the true nature of the intersection of spiritual phenomena with our physical dimension.

CHAPTER 1

What Is a UFO?

Almost everyone knows that the term UFO stands for Unidentified Flying Object. The term UFO is self-explanatory in that it refers to an unknown something flying in the sky or space. Essentially, it means a particular object in the sky can't be identified as a known aircraft, conventional celestial object, optical illusion, or a weather phenomenon. Anytime an unknown object is seen flying in the sky or space or tracked on radar, it's a UFO. Of course, that doesn't automatically mean it's from outer space or another dimension, it simply means it isn't identified . . . it's a UFO.

Common related terms include flying saucer, flying discs, or more recently, unidentified aerial phenomena (UAP). The United States government prefers the term UAP to UFO, so we will be seeing this term more frequently in the future. A UFO by any other name is still a UFO, so I will stick with that term for now. The term flying saucer originated from a private pilot's observation of a group of UFOs in 1947. He described the UFOs as moving through the sky like saucers skipping across water. From that description, the media coined the term flying saucers, which we still hear today. In reality, UFOs are observed in many shapes and sizes and have been described as an orb, saucer-shaped, cigar-shaped, triangle-shaped, tick-tack-shaped, etc. UFOs are often described as glowing or displaying various lights.

In addition to UFOs being observed in various shapes and sizes, they have been observed by many individuals and tracked by military technology to "fly" in the mediums of space, earth's atmosphere, and bodies of water. The term USO has been coined to describe Unidentified Submerged Objects that have been tracked at speeds underwater that exceed human technology. UFOs have been observed to enter and emerge from lake and ocean depths.

UFO observations and legends have been around for centuries. An internet search will reveal reports throughout history. Of course, ancient UFO sightings weren't called UFOs or flying saucers. They were described in contemporary terms familiar to the observers. Alexander the Great was said to have described an encounter with glowing "flying shields." The Hopi Indians also referred to "flying shields" and a sky god. Ancient Romans reported flying shields, fiery globes, ships, and stones.

A Roman report in 74 BC describes a large object shaped like a wine bottle and the color of molten silver that descended from the sky. The object came between two armies about to engage in battle. The armies were so astonished that they separated.

In 65 AD, Josephus, the Jewish historian, reported flying "chariots" seen hurtling through the clouds throughout Judea. UFOs are nothing new. In 2007, Richard Strothers, a NASA scientist, published a paper titled *Unidentified Flying Objects in Classical Antiquity.*[6] This work is a historical and scientific analysis of ancient UFO reports and compares them with modern UFO observations.

In 1975, David Jacobs, a university professor, published a book titled *The UFO Controversy in America*. The book deals with sightings from the 1890s to the 1970s. J. Allen Hyneck of Project Blue Book (see below) wrote the introduction to this work.

The key point to understand here is the fact that UFO observations are nothing new. Today, we have better technology available to investigate and document UFO encounters, but the U part of UFO remains the same as it was 2000 years ago. We have more information and documentation than ever, but UFOs remain *unidentified*. We have been observing and documenting them for years, but the question remains, "What is a UFO?" We can also ask, "Where do they come from?" and "Who or what is the intelligence behind them?"

In the United States there has been a tendency to write off, discount, or attribute UFO reports to misidentified natural phenomena, hysteria, hallucinations, or fraud. Individuals who have observed and reported UFOs have often been looked upon with suspicion or considered unreliable, perhaps because of an over-active imagination, mental disorder, or a fraudulent motive. No doubt many reported UFO sightings can be attributed to these causes. Given that UFO sightings and the observers themselves have often been treated with suspicion and skepticism, commercial pilots and military personnel have often been reluctant to report UFO incidents because it could have a negative impact on their record and even their career.

Despite this, there have always been a number of credible UFO sightings that defy scientific explanation. Many UFO sightings have been reported by highly credible witnesses— sometimes multiple credible witnesses and sometimes simultaneously confirmed by radar and other technology as well as visual documentation. The appearance, disappearance, and performance of many observed UFOs defy conventional explanation and exceed any known human technology.

The United States government has investigated UFO sightings off and on for years. From 1947 to 1969, the US Air Force investigated UFO reports through various projects culminating in what was known as Project Blue Book (1952–1969). When Project Blue Book was closed, it reported that the majority of UFO sightings could be explained, but a small number—a little over 5 percent of the reports—remained unexplained.

Unfortunately, some of Blue Book's explanations of UFO sightings lacked credibility, and when a credible UFO sighting in Michigan was attributed to "swamp gas," much of the public lost confidence in the government's investigations into UFOs. The term swamp gas came to symbolize the government's obfuscation of the UFO phenomenon. The government's historic propensity to dismiss, deny, and obfuscate reports of UFO sightings has caused some to say, "Don't believe anything about UFOs until it has been officially denied by the government." Unfortunately, the government has earned such cynicism.

In 1966, the government funded a project to investigate UFOs and Project Blue Book. The project was headed by a physicist by the name of Edward Condon. The Condon project generated a lot of internal conflict, but long before the project was completed, Condon declared that UFOs were "bunk." The conclusion of the Condon Report, written by Condon himself, said as much. The Condon Report conclusions were that UFOs did not appear to be a national threat, there was no evidence that they were extraterrestrial, and they exhibited no technology beyond current scientific knowledge. While the conclusions of the Condon Report were not accepted by many, including some involved in the project, it was decided that the UFO phenomenon did not warrant the expense of further investigation, and Project Blue Book was shut down.

It is worth noting that J. Allen Hynek, the lead civilian scientist involved in Project Blue Book, began his work with Blue Book as a UFO skeptic. In the course of his Blue Book investigations as well as subsequent investigations, he became convinced that UFOs were a real phenomenon worthy of serious study. Hynek disagreed with the conclusions of Project Blue Book and the Condon Report and was unhappy with the government's insistence on explaining UFOs away rather than seriously investigating them. He subsequently established an organization called the Center for UFO Studies (CUFOS) as a mechanism to report and study UFOs.

While the government's conclusion about UFOs from Project Blue Book and the Condon Report was essentially "There's nothing to see here folks, move along," the government did not lose interest in the UFO phenomenon. After Project Blue Book was shut down, the US government has continued to spend millions of dollars investigating UFOs or UAP. In 2017, the government admitted the existence of an unpublicized program that started in the Defense Intelligence Agency called the Advanced Aerospace Threat Identification Program (AATIP). AATIP ran from 2007 to 2012. AATIP was essentially an unclassified name for a twenty-two-million-dollar covert Defense Intelligence Agency program called the Advanced Aerospace Weapon System Application Program (AAWSAP). AAWSAP was funded for about two years, but AATIP continued a little longer. The stated objective of AAWSAP was to study and understand the threat potential and the physics and engineering of advanced aerospace weapon system applications that turned out to be government speak for studying UFOs or UAPs, as the government likes to call them. AAWSAP also investigated paranormal and psychic phenomena associated with UAPs. AAWSAP is described in more detail in the next chapter. As you read on, you will find there is significant paranormal—or I prefer the term spiritual—activity associated with UFOs.

AATIP was succeeded by a program in the Office of Naval Intelligence titled the Unidentified Aerial Phenomena Task Force (UAPTF). While government intelligence and Department of Defense agencies have continued to investigate and collect data on UFO/UAP incidents, the collected information has been classified or largely withheld from the public. In 2020, Congress required the UAPTF to produce an unclassified report on what it knows about the UFO/UAP phenomenon. This report is discussed in the next chapter. The report was to include an assessment of the phenomenon, including FBI investigations of UFO intrusion into restricted airspace around military installations and activity.

It appears both parties in Congress are weary of the secrecy around governmental UFO investigations and wanted an open, unclassified assessment for public consumption. I suspect the 2020 leaked release of military aircraft videos showing the tracking of UFOs is at least part of the reason Congress demanded an unclassified report for the public's right to know. UFOs were becoming an elephant in the living room, and the government's policy of denying, discounting, and misdirecting was increasingly seen as disingenuous and eroding credibility.

On one level, the United States government in general and the military in particular have appeared uninterested, dismissive, and secretive regarding UFO incidents. However, on another level, behind the scenes, they have been spending millions of taxpayer dollars investigating UFOs. As more and more reports of UFO encounters have become public, the government has lost more and more credibility as a result of their dismissive, secretive position on the UFO matter. The public, and apparently Congress, grew tired of this situation and demanded open revelation of what the government/military knows about UFOs. In the next chapter we will look at what the United States government is currently saying about UAPs in their unclassified report.

CHAPTER 2

What Does the Government Say about UFOs?

I n recent years, the media appears to be airing increased reports of UFO activity from military and governmental sources. Some of these reports have been leaked rather than officially released by the military. Traditionally, as described in the previous chapter, the government, including the military and some private agencies, have downplayed and/or failed to release full reports of incidents involving UFOs. As reports and evidence of UFO encounters have leaked out, the government has been under increased pressure to officially address the matter in a more forthright way and reveal what is known about UFOs.

As previously noted, the United States government has been studying the UFO phenomenon for many years. As pointed out in chapter 1, while the United States government has been publicly dismissive and secretive about the UFO phenomenon, at the same time it has taken the matter seriously enough to spend millions of tax dollars investigating UFOs. The public has grown increasingly weary of the government's elusive, secretive, and dismissive stance on UFOs, and finally, Congress acted.

In 2020, Congress required government agencies involved in UFO investigations to produce an unclassified report revealing what it knows about the UFO/UAP phenomenon. As a result, on June 25, 2021, the Director of National Intelligence released a nine-page unclassified document titled "Preliminary Assessment: Unidentified Aerial Phenomena." A classified document was also prepared but remains classified, presumably to protect military technology involved in UFO/UAP encounters.

The US government prefers to use the term Unidentified Aerial Phenomena or UAP as opposed to the more common term Unidentified Flying Object or UFO. The government has its own way of doing things and its own terminology. I suspect that, through the years, the term UFO has become culturally stigmatized, so the term UAP was coined to replace it. As the government becomes more open and involved in UFO investigations, I suspect the term UAP will eventually replace the more common term UFO. Hopefully, individuals who might be reluctant to be stigmatized by reporting a UFO observation will feel free to report a UAP, a government-sanctioned term for the same thing.

As an aside, I wonder if the UAP term will survive in the long run. It is often reported that UFOs or UAPs enter and exit from bodies of water. At least one governmental video shows a UAP entering and exiting a body of water at high speeds. No known human technology is capable of this. The term USO or Unidentified Submerged Object has already been coined. Perhaps the A—which stands for aerial—in UAP will have to be dropped, and the term will become UP for unidentified phenomenon. More likely a term like UTP will be used to stand for Unidentified Transmedia Phenomena. Time will reveal how the terminology evolves.

Given that the government, and particularly the military, has a proclivity to secrecy and a reluctance to say, "We don't know," I wasn't too optimistic about a completely candid official public UFO report or policy from the government. I anticipated that a governmental public report would be something innocuous like, "We don't know what they are at this time, but we believe it is something to be studied." That is essentially what the report said.

The public preliminary report was limited to reports—mostly from military aviators—between 2004 and 2021. A total of 144 reports from governmental agencies were reviewed, and all remain unidentified except one that was attributable to a large deflating balloon. A total of eighty of the reported observations involved observation or confirmation by multiple sensors such as radar, infrared, or conventional video, etc. This confirms that they were actual physical objects as opposed to some sort of light refraction or visual phenomena.

The report noted that the UAP phenomena appeared to cluster around military testing and training activities but acknowledged that this apparent clustering may be due to the presence of advanced sensor systems in operation. Perhaps advanced sensor systems are seeing what was there all along. It was also noted that sometimes the presence of UAPs interrupted ongoing military training operations.

The preliminary report, while lacking in detail, proposes that there is probably more than one explanation for UAP events. Five explanatory categories were proposed:

Airborne clutter: This would include unidentified or misidentified things like birds, balloons, airborne recreational vehicles like drones, etc.

Natural atmospheric phenomena: This would be natural phenomena such as ice crystals, thermal fluctuations, or any natural phenomena that might be unidentified or misidentified visually or on sensory systems like radar, etc.

US government or industry development programs: This would include airborne classified products and programs by US entities.

Foreign adversary systems: This would include technology deployed by China, Russia, or another nation.

Other: This is anything that doesn't fit into the other four categories.

Of the 144 UAP events considered by the report, one (the deflating balloon) fit into the "airborne clutter" category and all the rest fit into the "other" category.

One of the requirements of the report was to address the threat potential of the UAP phenomenon. The report affirmed the real threat of UAP to flight safety. It cited multiple near misses between UAP and military aircraft. The report also acknowledged the potential threat to US interests if UAPs represent advanced technology in the possession of hostile or potentially hostile foreign governments.

The entity within the Department of Defense that was tasked with investigating and coordinating the investigation of UAPs within the government at the time the report was released was the Unidentified Aerial Phenomena Task Force or UAPTF. It was announced in November 2021 that the UAPTF will be replaced by what was called the Airborne Object Identification and Management Synchronization Group (AOIMSG). Since the UAPTF was based in the navy, the new organizational entity was likely formed to coordinate UFO reporting and research across all Defense Department and other governmental agencies. It's unclear if the UAPTF within the navy structure will remain active. In any event, the Defense Department is gearing up to normalize, destigmatize, standardize, and enhance UAP reporting and investigation across military and all governmental entities.

I suspect the UFO or UAP investigative unit nomenclature within the Defense Department will evolve as they get more organized. Whoever came up with the name Airborne Object Identification and Management Synchronization Group is sure to be demoted for failing to come up with a name that lends itself to a short or pronounceable (SOP) acronym. AOIMSG doesn't exactly roll off the tongue. FYI, in our government and military, acronyms are SOP.

Our government has been spending millions of dollars investigating UFOs in public and secret programs for decades, but it appears that going forward, the UAPTF and/or the AOIMSG will be coordinating and consolidating the investigations of the UAP in a more systematic and open manner. Exactly how open the government will be remains to be seen.

Events Prior to the Release of the Preliminary Assessment: Unidentified Aerial Phenomena Report Required by Congress

In order to see the required public report (June 2021) in perspective, I think it is important to look at some events and government research preceding the report. It appears Congress required the public version of the report primarily in response to the recent release of military accounts and videos of UFO encounters. However, information about a prior and somewhat covert government research program was also coming to light. In December 2017, *The New York Times* released an article titled, "Glowing Auras and Black Money." It was in the context of the recent release of military UFO videos and information leaking out about a previous secret government study of UFOs that Senators Mark Rubio and Mark Warner on the Senate Intelligence Committee began to push for the public release of information about what the government knows about UFOs.

The Black Money project that *The New York Times* was referring to was a twenty-two-million-dollar government research program titled AAWSAP. Senators Harry Reid, Ted Stevens, and Dan Inouye allocated the funding for AAWSAP, which ran from 2007 into 2010. The primary objective of AAWSAP was to identify the threat potential of UFOs and to try to understand the advanced technology employed by UFOs.

Once funded, a government request for proposal was released, and Bigelow Aerospace Advanced Space Studies (BAASS) won the contract as the only bidder. Robert Bigelow has long been a government contractor associated with the United States space program. However, he has also had an interest in UFOs and related paranormal phenomena.

While AAWSAP was designed to study UFOs, the program cast a wide net to include psychic and paranormal phenomena related to the UFO phenomena. The AAWSAP study included research on what has become known as Skinwalker Ranch in northern Utah. The ranch and adjoining area have been a hotspot of UFO and paranormal activity for many years. Reports of UFO sightings in the area go back nearly 100 years. In 1996, Robert Bigelow learned of the reputation of the ranch and purchased it from the owner, who had many frightening stories to tell and was glad to sell it. Bigelow set up a variety of cameras and sensors and studied the ranch for years prior to his involvement in AAWSAP. The book *Skinwalkers at the Pentagon*, mentioned in the introduction, describes a number of disturbing events and observations taking place at the Skinwalker Ranch during the AAWSAP investigation. The AAWSAP investigation went far beyond the Skinwalker Ranch and documented other disturbing UFO and paranormal encounters that are reported in the book.

After the AAWSAP investigation concluded, Bigelow sold the Skinwalker Ranch, and ongoing investigations of UFO and paranormal activity are continuing under the new owner. Much of the ongoing investigation is documented in a History Channel TV series called *The Secret of Skinwalker Ranch*.

The UFO investigative program known as the AATIP was originally a function of AAWSAP but became independently known as AATIP while AAWSAP retained some anonymity. When AAWSAP ran out of funds and was shut down, AATIP continued to be funded, focusing on UFOs or UAPs, as they are known in the military. AATIP was succeeded by a unit in the Office of Naval Intelligence known as the UAPTF. In November 2021, UAPTF was succeeded by the AOIMSG in the Office of the Under Secretary of Defense for Intelligence and Security.

Is it just me, or is the constant renaming and repositioning of UFO-related investigations within our government and military beginning to look like a shell game? Perhaps it's more like a hot potato, but one does get the impression of obfuscation. Will the government ever be open and forthright with UFO investigations, or will they ultimately be delegated to the Department of Swamp Gas?

The required "Preliminary Assessment: Unidentified Aerial Phenomenon" report released in June 2021 addressed only military encounters with UFOs and did not go into the associated paranormal encounters involving UFOs as documented by AAWSAP. It turns out that a number of highly-placed government and military officials objected to AAWSAP's investigation into UFOs and associated paranormal activity. For reasons previously addressed, many people prefer to keep UFOs and associated phenomena at arm's length and don't want to be associated with such investigations. Some military personnel objecting to the study of UFOs, extraterrestrials, and related phenomena have been characterized as religious fanatics who feel it's all demonic or conflicts with their religious worldview. The study of UFOs and related phenomena is highly controversial at some levels within our government.

If someone inclined to associate UFOs and related phenomena with demonic activity is labeled a religious fanatic, I would, by that definition, be a religious fanatic. However, I don't necessarily object to the study of UFOs and related phenomena. I want the evidence open to the public. In my studies of the research conducted by the government and others, the demonic origin of UFOs and associated entities and phenomena can be firmly established. This connection of UFOs with the demonic can best be seen from the context of a biblical worldview. However, even without a biblical worldview, the connection can be made by informed individuals who are not locked into a materialist worldview. I fear for the secular researchers, locked into a secular worldview, who are deceived and outmatched in intellect and power when dealing with these deceptive phenomena.

I realize that associating UFOs with demonic activity is a bit of a leap and perhaps difficult to accept for some as I have not yet presented the evidence for this conclusion. However, I encourage the reader to continue reading to see the evidence on which this conclusion is based.

The government's "Preliminary Assessment: Unidentified Aerial Phenomena" report was inconclusive in that while it acknowledged the reality of UAP, it was unable to identify the source or essence of the phenomena. The phenomena remain unidentified. The acknowledgment of the physical reality of UAPs was, in itself, a significant public statement. The report provided no evidence that UAPs are extraterrestrial or technology from other nations on earth. However, it did not rule out these possibilities. Because of real or potential hazards to United

States interests, the thrust of the report was to propose comprehensive and coordinated reporting and investigation of UAPs.

Of course, there is always the remote possibility that UFOs or UAPs are a secret technology of the United States military. This seems unlikely, given we have been and are proposing the spending of millions of dollars investigating them. At least I'd like to think we wouldn't spend millions of tax dollars investigating ourselves. The idea that UFOs are a secret US technology, or the technology of any other nation, is also rendered improbable given that UFO phenomena were reported in history going back long before the United States or any current governmental entity existed.

CHAPTER 3

UFOs–An Awkward Reality

Misidentified natural phenomena, hallucinations, and fabrications aside, it is no longer possible to credibly deny the existence of UFOs. UFOs have been and are being observed by credible civilian and military witnesses and regularly tracked and filmed with objective civilian and military technology. Our government has been spending and continues to spend millions of dollars investigating UFOs because they are real, physical objects and documented to "fly" in space, in our atmosphere, and in bodies of water. They are documented to perform in ways well beyond our current understanding of physics and known human technology.

The big question today is no longer whether UFOs exist. As previously noted, the burning question is "what" and "who" are they? This is where the reality of UFOs gets awkward. An unconventional phenomenon requires an unconventional explanation. Any attempt to identify the "what" or "who" of UFOs takes one out of the box and outside of the comfort zone of known science and conventional human experience. Outside the bounds of known science and conventional reality, one is left with unconventional and uncomfortable speculations as to the "what" and "who" of UFOs.

Given that UFOs are an unconventional phenomenon without a current conventional explanation, we are compelled to consider unconventional explanations. The awkward reality is that any attempt to explain UFOs and/or aliens outside of conventional knowledge and understanding places one in an intellectual never-never land where one is potentially marginalized, stigmatized, or ridiculed. The starting place in any discussion of UFOs is outside of conventional or familiar reality. It stretches, if not strains, our sensibilities. I could call it an inconvenient truth, but that expression has already been used to take us in an entirely different direction.

Given that identification of the "what" and "who" of the UFO phenomenon takes one into unconventional and intellectually vulnerable territory, it's no wonder many people have ignored them or denied their existence. It can be awkward to admit UFOs exist because it is an admission of the existence of an unconventional reality with unconventional implications. Normal people don't usually talk about UFOs, do they?

There is a long history of people being ridiculed, marginalized, or stigmatized upon reporting an observation or encounter with a UFO. In a sense, UFOs tend to be a third rail that is to be avoided. This is true within the general public as well as with individuals in the military in this country. Accordingly, it has often been easier and safer to ignore and not express an opinion regarding UFOs. Likewise, individuals observing a UFO have found it expedient not to report the event in order to avoid the associated stigma and controversy. Obviously, ignoring the issue does not make it go away. The UFO phenomenon is forcing its way into contemporary reality, making it difficult to ignore. The government says they are real, and they are frequently in the news and with video documentation. Where once claiming belief in UFOs placed one into an intellectual fringe status, now denying the existence of UFOs is becoming a fringe position. They are here, they are real, the government admits it, and we have significant evidence.

The stigma connected to reporting a UFO observation is linked to a history of obviously fraudulent reports and reported encounters by individuals seeking publicity or suffering from a mental disorder. Many reported UFO sightings turn out to be misidentified conventional aircraft or other natural phenomena. Add to this the fact that some reports by credible witnesses often seem incredible by the standards of known science and technology. How does a credible witness retain credibility while describing an observed or experienced incredible phenomenon?

With witnesses who are not credible as well as credible witnesses both reporting incredible events and observations, the whole UFO phenomenon can be confusing and difficult to sort out. In the haze of credible and incredible UFO reports by credible and not so credible witnesses, it's no wonder so many people find it expedient to keep the whole subject at arm's length. Credible witnesses can be reluctant to report incredible observations in order to protect their credibility and avoid being stigmatized as one who "sees UFOs."

In broad terms, there have been three speculations offered as to the "what" and "who" of the UFO phenomenon. There are variations and flavors of each option, but they broadly fall into three categories. One explanation is somewhat conventional but highly improbable, and two explanations are well beyond the conventional and, to one degree or another, strain our sensibilities. The explanations offered fall into these three general categories:

1. UFOs are the product of unknown secret human technology.
2. UFOs are the product of extraterrestrial intelligences visiting earth.
3. UFOs are from another dimension (physical or spiritual).

Apart from the first speculation, the other two are outside of conventional knowledge and push into what can be perceived as science fiction, paranormal, and even religious territory. They are beyond conventional secular reality and are intellectually dangerous hot buttons.

The first option is the most conventional but least likely explanation for the UFO phenomenon. I say least likely because

UFOs in the present and distant past display flight and performance capabilities that exceed any known human technology. UFOs appear and disappear at will from visual sight and radar tracking. They fly with no obvious source of propulsion, with no aerodynamic configuration or flight-control surfaces. They also perform maneuvers that would produce g-forces that exceed known aircraft structural integrity and would be fatal to human occupants. A human can stand a g-force of 9Gs for a short period of time, and an F-16 fighter can withstand up to around 17Gs before coming apart. UFOs have been observed to perform maneuvers with g-forces measured in the thousands. The world's fastest jet planes currently have a top speed under 3,000 miles per hour. At least one plane under development is expected to exceed 4,000 miles per hour. The "tic tac" UFOs tracked by our military in 2004 dropped from an altitude of 28,000 feet to just above the surface of the ocean in less than a second when approached by navy aircraft launched from the USS Nimitz. This computes to somewhere above 18,000 miles per hour. When approached by navy aircraft, a UFO sped off in excess of 24,000 miles per hour. (This according to recorded interviews of Kevin Day, the now-retired Naval officer who was the chief radar operator on board the USS Princeton when tracking the UFOs and the pursuing navy aircraft.)

UFOs have been tracked to fly into, under, and out of water without observed performance deterioration. They accelerate to supersonic speeds without a sonic boom. On top of this, they have been observed to divide into two or more separate crafts. Multiple UFOs are sometimes observed to combine into one while in flight. There is no known man-made craft capable of this. Our government currently denies that UFOs are USA technology but refuses to rule out the possibility that they are technology from another earthly government or of extra-terrestrial origin.

One would have to ask, why would our government spend millions of dollars investigating reports of our own technology? If we invented them, why would we be investigating them? UFO reports go back hundreds of years before modern technology. Our government has been tracking and investigating UFOs since the 1940s. Is it reasonable to think that our government, or any government, could keep UFO technology secret this long? The military branches of several countries besides the United States are and have been investigating the UFO phenomenon. Is it reasonable to think any country in the world had UFO technology eighty years ago? For that matter, UFOs have been reported in history for over two thousand years, well before humans even imagined such technology.

With the collapse of the USSR, the US was able to see Russian intelligence on UFOs, and they are as clueless as we are about what they are and their origin. UFO technology exceeds our current human capabilities and understanding of physics. There is no hint of anything approaching UFO technology in any other country in the world.

If we eliminate option 1, i.e., that UFOs are unknown, secret human technology, we are left with two unconventional and intellectually uncomfortable options: they are extraterrestrial or extradimensional. These options are awkward to say the least. The social and theological implications are massive. We will look at these options in succeeding chapters.

CHAPTER 4

Why Extraterrestrial?

A s the media continues to address the UFO phenomenon, we are increasingly hearing UFOs referred to as "extra-terrestrial." That is, they are not of this planet. Commentators and people interviewed regarding UFO incidents frequently use the term extraterrestrial or expressions like "not of this world" when describing UFO crafts and/or the apparent performance and technology involved.

In the context of our culture today, the supposition of an extraterrestrial origin for UFOs makes sense. In fact, it's almost an inevitable or inescapable conclusion given the prevailing scientific and philosophical worldview assumptions at play in our culture. I will explain.

For years the public has been presented with books, TV programs, and movies featuring flying saucers, spaceships, UFOs, and various space aliens. The popular *Star Trek* TV and movie series along with movies like the *Star Wars* series, *Close Encounters of the Third Kind*, *Men in Black*, and *Contact* have saturated the public with stories of extraterrestrial beings and technology. These science-fiction programs routinely feature a wide variety of extraterrestrial entities with technologies that far exceed anything existing on earth today.

Have Life Forms Evolved on Other Planets?

A usually unstated but inherent supposition in all these science-fiction programs is the idea that life evolved by natural processes here on earth, so it must have evolved elsewhere in the universe. There is no need to explain the existence of extraterrestrial races or life forms in these movies because the naturalistic evolution of life in the universe is an assumed reality. I suspect that most of us have heard scientists or scholars make statements affirming that life must certainly have evolved elsewhere in this vast universe. For certain, we have all been told and taught through public education and the popular media that life evolved here on earth by entirely natural processes. This is not something that has been proved by science, but it is an underlying presupposition of secular origins doctrine that is taught and presented as confirmed science in the public education system and the popular media.

The strength of evolutionary theory in our culture is not founded on confirming science—it's found in philosophical naturalism, a belief system or worldview that has been conflated with the discipline of science and promoted in the public education system and popular media. Within this naturalistic worldview, naturalistic evolution is the only possible explanation for the origin of the universe and life within it. Concepts of creation and design are philosophically at odds with the prevailing naturalistic worldview and are therefore systematically disallowed, ignored, or marginalized in public education, many governmental institutions, and the media. The secular culture has captured the creation versus evolution origins debate in terms of religion versus science in order to win the origins debate by definition before the scientific data are considered.

When philosophical naturalism is applied to the UFO phenomenon, once an earth origin is ruled out, a naturalistic extraterrestrial evolutionary origin becomes a logical deduction. If the data rules out an earthly origin for UFOs and their associated sentient entities, then it follows that they are from somewhere else. Since creation and intelligent design are philosophically unacceptable alternatives, then somewhere else must be another planet with a habitable environment.

Along with many scholars and scientists, I am of the opinion that the origin of life by undirected natural processes (i.e., evolution) is utterly impossible on earth or anywhere else in the universe. I have written a book titled *Why I Am a Creationist* addressing the impossibility of the naturalistic origin of life by evolution, and there are many books by qualified scientists in many disciplines refuting the naturalistic origin of life. In order for life to exist, there are many properties of matter and energy that must be exactly right. Add to this the many requirements about the size of our planet, distance from our sun, position in our galaxy, and many other conditions required to permit life to exist.

Many scientists, even evolutionary scientists, marvel that the laws of physics and the environmental conditions on earth appear finely tuned to permit life to exist. Even with fortuitously fine-tuned physics and optimum boundary conditions for life to exist, the possibility that life could evolve into existence by time, chance, and chemistry is still nil. The complex information content in living biological systems is massive and far beyond the capability of chance and chemistry under any time frame or conditions. I don't intend to argue the creation versus evolution debate here. The main point I am making is that if you begin with the assumption that life evolved into existence on earth by natural processes, it is not unreasonable to consider that life evolved elsewhere in this vast universe where the conditions might be right.

In spite of the fact that the naturalistic origin of life is an assumption rather than demonstrable science, a significant portion of our culture accepts the naturalistic origin and evolution of life as a matter of "proven" science. The naturalistic evolution of life is more than an assumption—it is a fundamental element of the worldview of many in our culture. Out of this assumption and worldview, the idea of extraterrestrial life is perceived to be at least a possibility if not a probability.

When the UFO phenomenon is examined within the context of prevailing scientific and evolutionary worldview assumptions, the extraterrestrial hypothesis is almost inevitable. After all, UFOs are often observed to be under intelligent control and interacting with their environment. They have performance characteristics and technology that exceed anything possible on earth by man-made technology. They have been tracked at 25,000 miles per hour on radar, and they instantly accelerate to speeds in excess of 7,000 miles per hour. They have been observed to make sudden stops or right angle turns at over 15,000 miles per hour. The g-forces associated with such maneuvers would be fatal to human passengers and exceed the structural integrity of any man-made craft. They appear and disappear from human sight and radar and divide into multiple crafts, morph into different shapes, and fly in and out of bodies of water without breaking apart. When on the ground, UFOs have been known to leave indentions, radiation, and scorching as if they are actual physical objects, but in the air, they often appear to perform as if they have no mass. There is no human technology on earth capable of these feats.

I should emphasize that, in this chapter, I am using the term extraterrestrial to refer to a planet, star system, galaxy, or any celestial location other than earth. I am distinguishing between extraterrestrial and extradimensional. By extraterrestrial I am referring to a physical location in our universe on a planet or planets other than earth.

If UFO performance exceeds the ability of any technology on earth, then where do they come from? Given cultural assumptions, it can be concluded that they must have come from somewhere other than earth and that, by definition, means they are extraterrestrial. It's almost humorous to hear military officials interviewed about UFO performance and origins because many are reluctant to use the word extraterrestrial, so they will say something like "out of this world" or "not of this world." Nevertheless, the term extraterrestrial is increasingly heard and is an unavoidable consideration, if not a logical conclusion, given prevailing cultural assumptions.

In summary, the frequent, if not common identification of UFOs as extraterrestrial visitors makes total sense if you begin with the assumption of the naturalistic evolutionary origin of life on earth. If life evolved naturally here on earth, then why not elsewhere in the vast universe? The fact that UFO technology is observed to exceed any known earthly technology is seen as evidence of the extraterrestrial origin of UFOs. I will discuss it in more detail later, but I should note here that the extraterrestrial (ET) or alien entities associated with the UFO phenomenon often tell earth contactees that they are from another planet or star system.

Practical Arguments Against the Extraterrestrial Hypothesis

Apart from the fact that science is unable to demonstrate that life did or could evolve on earth, is it realistic to think of UFOs and ET as coming from another planet, star system, or galaxy? (This subject is discussed in detail in chapter 2 of the book *Alien Intrusion*—recommended in the introduction.) There are time, distance, and physical obstacles that would seem to preclude UFOs from visiting from another planet. For starters, there are no habitable planets in our solar system, so ET would have to come from farther out in space. The next closest star to earth is 4.2 light years away. A light year is a measure of distance—the distance light can travel in a year. Traveling at 186,000 miles per second (the speed of light), it would take 4.2 years to reach the next nearest star, and who knows if it has a habitable planet in orbit?

Traveling at the speed of light is problematic because as mass approaches the speed of light it becomes infinite. It would take infinite energy to move an infinite-mass spacecraft at the speed of light and then more infinite energy to stop it if you could. This raises obvious fuel and propulsion issues. It would take 100,000 years to cross our galaxy at the speed of light. Traveling from another galaxy is even more problematic for ET because even at the speed of light it would take over 25,000 years to arrive from the next closest galaxy. Traveling at less than the speed of light only exacerbates the time/distance problem.

Traveling through space is also problematic because space is not empty. It is estimated that there are 100,000 dust particles per cubic kilometer (about 25 percent of a cubic mile) in space. The EU-funded CODITA project (Cosmic Dust in the Terrestrial Atmosphere) concluded that forty-three tons of space dust enters our atmosphere every day. Traveling at one-tenth the speed of light, an impact with a dust particle would have the kinetic energy of ten tons of TNT. It's not likely you could detect a dust particle in your path at any speed, let alone the speed of light, and any turning movement to avoid it would put millions of g-forces on the spacecraft and passengers. Even if the craft could withstand the g-forces, the occupants would end up a thin mist on the walls after a turn at any speed approaching lightspeed.

If it would take forty-two years at one-tenth the speed of light to reach the next closest star from ours, that seems a long time to risk impact with dust particles in space. An eighty-four-year round trip would double the hazard, require a lot of supplies, and necessitate a long lifespan or a multi-generational voyage. It's difficult to imagine ET having such an intense interest in visiting earth that he would be willing to travel decades to visit us and then avoid direct contact with us.

Given our current understanding of physics, it's not likely that ET is coming and going from another planet. The time and distance and space dust obstacles are insurmountable. Of course, you can invoke warped space, wormholes, and the handy warp-drive available on the Starship Enterprise and the Millennium Falcon to resolve the time/distance obstacles, but then there's reality.

Theological Arguments Against the Extraterrestrial Hypothesis

We will discuss the theological implications of the extraterrestrial origin of UFOs in greater detail in subsequent chapters, but I have pointed out here that the assumption of the naturalistic origin and evolution of life on earth facilitates belief in the naturalistic origin of life elsewhere in the universe. The

UFO phenomenon and associated ET entities reinforce belief in extraterrestrial life and at the same time reinforce and build on the assumption of the naturalistic evolutionary origin of life on earth. From the secularist perspective, UFOs may be evidence that humans are just one of many sentient life forms in the universe. This secular perspective marginalizes the God of the Bible who didn't mention ET and is laboring under the opinion that He created the heavens and earth and all life.

The God of the Bible has said that He created mankind in His image, and the biblical record deals primarily with God and His relationship with mankind on earth. The Bible does not talk about God creating life on other planets. How is the secular person to perceive the God of the Bible and human beings if he or she comes to believe that we humans are just one of many sentient life forms in the universe? Is the Christian church prepared to fit UFOs and ET into a biblical worldview?

Of course, Christians who chose to believe in extraterrestrial entities will likely say that, if they exist, they were created by God. This thinking is partly consistent with a biblical worldview because God did create everything (Genesis 1:1; John 1:3; Colossians 1:16). However, Scripture tells us that God created angels and then human and animal life on earth. We are not told anything about God creating ET life on other planets. Scripture tells us that mankind was created in the image of God (Genesis 1:27), but it doesn't mention anything about creating extraterrestrials or whose image they might be in.

Scripture—and particularly the Genesis record—clearly depicts man as the centerpiece of all creation. God created the earth to provide for man's needs (Isaiah 45:18) and gave mankind dominion over all earthly creatures (Genesis 1:26–29). Even the sun, moon, and stars are created for our benefit (Genesis 1:14–18). This is not an egocentric view originating with mankind; it's our Creator's description of reality.

With Adam's sin came the fall of man described in Genesis 3. The fall brought death (Genesis 2:17; Romans 5:12, 6:23) and corruption into God's once perfect creation. All nature fell with mankind (Genesis 3:17–19; Romans 8:20–22) and is under the curse of sin until the new heaven and earth arrive (Revelation 21). This means that if extraterrestrials exist, they are fallen creatures, like humans, in a fallen creation.

To provide mankind a path to reconciliation and salvation, God in His amazing grace, in the person of Jesus Christ, became a man to die for the sins of mankind (Romans 5:8, 17–19). Christ died for the sins of mankind and paid the price, so that we, by faith in Christ, can obtain forgiveness for our sins and receive eternal life. God did not become an angel or extraterrestrial to die for angels or ET. If ETs exist, they are fallen creatures and, like fallen angels, outside of God's plan of salvation. Humans who claim to have contact with ETs should bear this in mind when ET shares his theology.

The Extraterrestrial Hypothesis Is Both Logical and Improbable

My point in this chapter is that our culture is programmed by a pervasive naturalistic worldview and associated evolutionary theory to conclude that UFOs, and any associated entities, are the product of naturalistic evolution on another planet. The performance and technology demonstrated by UFOs exceed anything known on earth. Accordingly, we see the media and various individuals referring to UFOs as an "extraterrestrial" phenomenon. This is a logical conclusion in the context of the prevailing naturalistic worldview. Of course, if life didn't and couldn't evolve into existence by natural processes on earth, all bets are off.

While the extraterrestrial hypothesis is logical in one context, it is improbable in the context of certain scientific and theological considerations. Time, distance, propulsion, and energy requirements make travel from another solar system or galaxy impractical if not impossible. Add to this the hazard of collision with particles of space debris while in transit, and the extraterrestrial idea is even less probable.

The idea that life evolved by natural processes anywhere in the universe, let alone on earth, is also problematic. The naturalistic evolution of life is philosophically the only game in town, but scientifically it remains unproven and statistically impossible. Life requires a creator, but the rules of philosophical naturalism preclude such a consideration. While the naturalistic origin of extraterrestrial life is philosophically possible, it is scientifically impossible.

If UFOs and associated sentient entities don't come from earth and can't reasonably come from another star system or galaxy, then where do they come from? We will discuss this in the next chapter.

CHAPTER 5

Do UFOs Come from Another Dimension?

In the previous chapter we looked at theological and scientific reasons that UFOs and their associated entities are not likely visitors from another planet. If not a product of earthly technology or technology from another planet, we must consider the possibility that UFOs are from another dimension. When we talk about UFOs and ETs coming from another dimension, we need to define what we mean by another dimension. This can be complicated and can require us to draw on science, theology, and our imagination.

Let's start by thinking about our universe, which has four dimensions that we are all familiar with. The four familiar dimensions we live in are width, height, length, and time. This is sometimes referred to as the time-space continuum. A horizontal line exists in only one dimension because it only has length. Draw a square, and you have two dimensions: width and length. Draw or imagine a cube, and you have three dimensions: width, height, and length. Time is a fourth dimension that we live in and are familiar with.

Time is a little deceptive because we think of time as flowing evenly from past to present to future. We live in the present, the past is behind us, and the future is ahead of us. That's how we perceive and experience time, and it works for us. Time, however, is relative and an integral part of our physical space-time universe. Time varies or is influenced by gravity and velocity. Gravity bends time and space, and at the speed of light, time stands still. Nevertheless, from our fixed perspective here on earth, time is perceived and experienced in a steady, familiar, linear way.

I should add that God is not bound by time as we are. God is the creator of our space-time universe, so He transcends both time and space. While outside of time and space as we know it, God acts and deals with us within our physical space and time frame to accomplish his purposes.

Some scientists dealing with the physics of string theory maintain that there are a number of additional invisible dimensions beyond the four that are familiar to us. These additional dimensions aren't well defined, but they make the math work. I point this out only to note that it's difficult to conceive of UFOs coming into our familiar dimensional universe from another dimensional framework. When UFOs appear to us in our time and in our three-dimensional space, they are themselves three-dimensional with width, height, and length, giving them a conventional shape. It's difficult to conceive of them as three-dimensional craft coming from or returning to another dimensional environment.

I think that most people who think of UFOs as being hyper-dimensional or coming from another dimension think of them as coming from a parallel dimensional universe similar in some respect to ours. There are theories or conjectures that propose additional universes, but no known parallel universe has been detected and known to science.

Could there be another dimensional universe, unexplored by science, that is not part of or separate from the dimensions of our known universe? We could confuse this whole subject even more by supposing UFOs come from this universe but from a different time dimension. Whatever dimensional origin may be involved, we encounter UFOs in our time frame and in our four-dimensional universe.

Mankind's knowledge of science runs a little thin when we try to imagine UFOs coming from another invisible universe or time dimension. However, the very existence of UFOs and their amazing performance, along with their unidentified creators and operators, are already beyond mankind's scientific knowledge. UFOs are an unconventional phenomenon, and it's reasonable to anticipate an unconventional explanation.

This brings us to another dimensional consideration. There is a dimension that almost all cultures around the world recognize in one way or another, but a dimension which science has not defined or explored in any detail. I'm talking about a spiritual dimension. All religions are based on a spiritual dimension or reality apart from our familiar observable, measurable, testable, four-dimensional universe. The concept of a spiritual dimension is almost innate in humanity. Almost all cultures around the world have beliefs or traditions that may involve spirits, ghosts, and/or an afterlife. We experience our physical existence and reality, but we seem to "know" there's something more. As Ecclesiastes 3:11 puts it, God "has put eternity into man's heart." We humans tend to be religious and most, if not all, religions involve a spiritual dimension, including life beyond life on earth.

When we consider UFOs as coming from a spiritual dimension, I will bring us back to the biblical worldview, which is founded in the infallible world of the God of all creation. The Bible speaks of unseen places or locations in a spiritual dimension such as Heaven and Hell. The Bible also speaks of largely unseen entities such as angels and demons and God himself who dwells in a spiritual dimension but also dwells and acts within our dimensional framework.

The God of the Bible is the creator of our familiar dimensional universe. From time to time throughout history, God, angels, and demons have appeared physically and interacted with humanity in our familiar physical universe. UFOs and associated ETs also appear to be trans-dimensional as they pop in and out of our physical universe just as angels and demons do. After all, UFOs go someplace when we aren't seeing them. From the context of a Christian-biblical worldview, we know that there is traffic between our familiar physical universe and the spiritual dimension.

Historically, cultures around the world have reports and traditions involving gods, ghosts, and spiritual entities visiting and interacting with humans. These reports are often manifested in religious views and traditions and legends, but they demonstrate that trans-dimensional interactions and beliefs are common to humanity. It's not unreasonable to consider that an almost universal concept of a spiritual dimension has some basis in reality.

Perhaps we can think of ourselves in our physical universe as a lesser included part of a greater invisible spiritual universe or dimension around us. I sometimes think of our physical universe as something like a temporal island in a greater eternal spiritual dimension. This idea is captured in 2 Corinthians 4:18 when Paul says, "The things that are seen are transient but the things that are unseen are eternal." In an online sermon that touched on this verse, I heard scientist and theologian Chuck Missler refer to the visible physical world as something like virtual reality while the invisible (spiritual) world is the eternal "real world." To emphasize this point, he pointed out that most of the matter in this world is empty space. Matter in our physical universe is made up of atoms, but atoms are 99.9 percent empty space. Anything we see as solid is actually mostly empty space, so in a sense, we do live in a virtual reality. God, who created everything, created us and our physical universe within the context of His plans and purposes. While God, angels, and demons have access to our physical universe, we don't have access to the spiritual universe as long as we are living in our physical bodies.

In his comedy, *As You Like It,* Shakespeare wrote the line, "All the world's a stage." While not necessarily intended by Shakespeare, perhaps this expression can depict the relationship of our physical dimensional universe within the context of a greater eternal spiritual dimension. Our physical world is something like a temporal stage created by God on which to demonstrate His power, justice, grace, and mercy. Our world is also a stage on which much of a great spiritual battle is played out as God and Satan battle for the souls of mankind. God has provided mankind access to salvation by coming into our dimensional world and dying on the cross to pay the penalty for our sin. He has also equipped us with the Word of Truth (the Bible), like a script to show us our role and relationship to God on this world stage. While God offers salvation through faith in the person and work of Christ, Satan and his demonic allies attempt to distract and deceive us. All of this is played out on our transient world stage.

The logical question at this point is, "Why would we consider UFOs to be coming from the spiritual dimension?" This is an important question, and the answer is even more important. Every Bible-believing Christian should be aware that mankind, and our physical universe, is center stage in an ongoing spiritual battle between God and a powerful fallen angel called Satan, who is also called the god of this world (2 Corinthians 4:4).

Let's remind ourselves of who Satan is. Satan, also called the devil or Lucifer, which means light bearer, was originally created as Lucifer, a powerful, high-ranking, beautiful angel (Ezekiel 28:14–15). Lucifer, however, rebelled against God and became Satan and was cast out of Heaven along with a number of other rebellious angels (Revelation 12:4,7–9; Isaiah 14:12–15).

It's important to keep some theological issues in mind when we think about Satan. First, God did not create Satan; God created Lucifer, who by his prideful and rebellious will became Satan. God is eternal and self-existent, but Satan is not. Lucifer was created with a free will just as we have. In his pride, Lucifer chose the path of rebellion and became Satan. Like many rebels, Satan recruited others, and up to a third of the angels followed him in his rebellion. God threw Satan and his rebel angels from Heaven, and their eternal destiny is in Hell. Just as Satan recruited many angels to follow him in his rebellion, he and his demons are doing their best to corrupt mankind, turn us away from God, and thwart God's plan for mankind. The bulk of the Satanic and demonic activity on earth has been to attack, lead, mislead, distract, and direct mankind away from God's plan of salvation described in the paragraph below.

In chapter 3 of Genesis, we read that Satan acted deceptively, lied to Adam and Eve, and caused them to sin by disobeying God. This original sin is referred to as the fall of man and has had terrible consequences for all mankind and nature itself that are still with us today (Genesis 3:1–19). Sin broke Adam and Eve's close personal relationship with God. God's original creation was perfect, but along with the fall came suffering, death, and decay (Romans 8:20–22). All mankind after Adam have inherited a sin nature and, along with that, death (Romans 5:12), suffering, and decay which are part of our existence in this fallen world. Every human being today is a sinner before God and in need of salvation, because sin results in death (Romans 6:23). However, God has provided a remedy for man's sin and a path to salvation and eternal life through His grace and our personal faith in the person and work of His son, Jesus Christ. The penalty for sin is death, and we are all sinners, but Christ took our sins on Himself and died on a cross in our place to pay the penalty we deserve (2 Corinthians 5:21). This amazing salvation is available to all by faith in Christ alone (John 11:25; John 14:6; Acts 4:12; Ephesians 2:8).

The destiny of Satan and his demonic cohort is Hell, but they will not be rulers in Hell; they will suffer with all unbelievers in eternity. God has provided a plan of salvation for fallen humans, but not for Satan and the fallen angels. All who read this have a free will to believe and receive God's salvation in Christ Jesus or to ignore it—choose wisely.

Satan is a lying, deceiving demon (John 8:44; 1 Peter 5:8; Ephesians 6:12) and engaged in spiritual warfare against God and his plan of salvation for mankind, starting in Genesis chapter 3 where he lied to and deceived Adam and Eve and brought about the fall of mankind (Ezekiel 28:13; Genesis 3:1–5). Satan and his fallen angel-demons often try to appear as angels of light to deceive humans and thwart God's plans (2 Corinthians 11:14–15).

So why am I associating UFOs with Satan and his fallen angel-demons? I am not associating UFOs and ET with satanic entities just because they are strange, difficult to explain, and exceed human technology. The satanic linkage is easy and logical once you understand who the supposed extraterrestrial entities associated with UFOs are and who they say they are. UFOs have demonstrated themselves to be under intelligent control, so the burning question has been, who is the intelligence? Who is behind the UFO phenomenon, and what is their intention? We are not left to guess about who the entities associated with UFOs are. They have identified themselves, and we will explore this in the following chapters.

CHAPTER 6

UFOs, Abductions, and Abductees

In this chapter, for convenience, I will refer to the entities associated with UFOs as aliens or ETs. By ET I mean extraterrestrial, but not from another planet. I am using ET to identify the entities associated with UFOs as not originating from earth, i.e., this planet. As noted in the previous chapter, I am associating UFO-connected ETs as coming from a spiritual dimension. My determination for this contention is based in large part on how ET has identified himself and revealed his theology.

In one sense, the UFOs in our skies and waters are a distraction. Our government and other governments around the world see these signs and wonders and want to know who they are, what are their intentions, and how can we get ahold of this amazing technology? For the most part, governments and individuals are seeking to understand UFOs scientifically but not spiritually. While governments are investigating the physical phenomena of UFOs, there is a worldwide record of encounters between humans and entities associated with UFOs who claim to be extraterrestrial aliens visiting from distant star systems and galaxies.

This brings us to the subject of alien/ET close encounters, visitations, and abductions. (Can you hear the theme from the TV series *The Twilight Zone* in the background?) In the past, I have discounted claims and reports of close encounters and abductions involving aliens and UFOs. I attributed such reports to people seeking attention or suffering from some sort of psychological aberration. I suspect many, if not most, people have done the same thing. To be sure, there is no shortage of fraudulent reports of alien-human contact by people with deceptive motives or by individuals seeking publicity. On closer examination, it turns out these human-alien encounters and events are a worldwide phenomenon and are happening to a wide variety of people. It has been estimated, based on a 1991 Roper poll, that nearly four million Americans have suffered from an alien-abduction experience. On top of this, there are thousands of individuals and groups around the world actively seeking contact with UFOs and aliens.

We will discuss the alien-abduction experience in the next chapter, but as an aside, I should note that UFOs are often associated with phenomena such as crop circles and cattle mutilations. This association is not well documented, and it's difficult to sort out fact from fraud or fiction in these cases. However, when humans interface with UFO-associated aliens, we have thousands of witnesses to give us details about their "close encounter." It is from these individuals we will learn who ET is.

What Are the UFOs Themselves?

As previously mentioned, UFOs come in various shapes and sizes and have been around for centuries. In recent years they have been observed by many credible witnesses and photographed, documented, and tracked with sophisticated military and civilian tracking technology. However, UFOs don't play by the rules of physics as we know them. They appear and disappear at will, visually or on radar. They accelerate, decelerate, and turn at speeds that exceed human technology. They accelerate to hypersonic speeds without a sonic boom. They experience g-forces that exceed the structural integrity of man-made aircraft that would be fatal for human beings.

They fly in and out of bodies of water, sometimes at speeds that would destroy any human-made craft. They leave indentations and evidence of weight when on the ground, but they often fly as if weightless. They fly with no known means of propulsion and without aerodynamic control surfaces. UFOs often change shape, divide into multiple crafts, or converge into a single craft.

While it is often proposed that UFOs are technology from another star or galaxy, I have pointed out the problems of space debris, time, distance, propulsion, and energy requirements that render this option impractical if not impossible. Of course, one can propose time and space warps, wormholes, and such to try to solve the practicalities of interstellar space travel. However, given the physics-defying performance of UFOs and the need to call upon extreme theoretical physics to imagine how they might regularly visit us from another star system or galaxy, perhaps we should consider that they aren't what they appear to be.

Perhaps UFOs are extradimensional paraphysical objects. That is, they are able to enter our dimensional universe as actual physical objects in one form but exist as invisible energy in another form. According to physics, matter and energy are interchangeable. What we see as a solid object (matter) is ultimately just a form of energy. UFOs are clearly physical objects with weight and mass in some cases, but at other times they appear translucent, and sometimes they "poof"—disappear or appear.

I'm not the first to propose that UFOs are paraphysical objects shifting between matter and energy or that they are visiting from another dimension. However, this makes sense when you realize that the UFO/alien phenomenon has a spiritual agenda, and the dimension from which they come is a spiritual dimension.

Through the years as I read UFO reports or heard individuals interviewed in the media, long before I began my personal study of the phenomena, it appeared to me that the appearance and performance of UFOs often seemed strange. It seemed as if their appearance and behavior were often almost like a show to attract attention. Whether appearing to an individual, a group of people, or an entire city, it seemed like they wanted to be noticed. It seems these appearances are intended to acclimate humans to the presence and reality of UFOs. I have come to believe this is intentional in many cases—a sign or show of technology beyond human science and ability to give ET and his message credibility when contact is made.

Are Alien Abductions Really Happening?

I will answer question this with a qualified *Yes*. It's happening to millions of people. To the individual themselves, it is *very* real and usually terrifying. When an individual recalls the abduction or re-experiences the event in hypnotic regression, they often express real fear and terror with dramatic emotional and physical reactions. Sometimes the experiencer's reaction to reliving the experience is so traumatic and terrifying that the hypnotic regression session must be terminated. Psychologists acknowledge that the individual describing the abduction truly believes it's real, and they are not making up a story.

Needless to say, the stories that abductees recount are unbelievable in the context of the conventional world and the concept of reality we are familiar with. Abductees are usually credible witnesses recounting an incredible experience. Some psychologists who specialize in treating abductees have come to believe the abduction experiences are real events experienced by the abductee. Other psychologists believe the abductee believes the event was real but attribute the experience to a psychological aberration of some sort. Since many abductees report that they are rendered immobile or paralyzed at points during the abduction, some psychologists diagnose it as a form of a sleep-paralysis syndrome. However, sometimes two individuals are abducted at once and give similar stories of the experience, making sleep paralysis an unlikely explanation. Sleep paralysis doesn't explain how two people could have the same experience at the same time, nor does it explain the worldwide similarities in the abduction experiences.

Do I think people are actually being kidnapped by space aliens and taken aboard spacecraft? I'll have to answer with

No, but then I will weasel my no by qualifying it. UFOs are clearly physical objects on some occasions, but they don't always behave as physical objects ought on other occasions. I answered the abduction question with a qualified *yes* earlier, but my qualification is this: Something real is happening, and individuals are experiencing what they perceive to be an abduction by aliens, but for reasons I have already stated, I don't believe the aliens are space aliens. The "something real" that is happening, I believe, is a demonic encounter with entities from the spiritual dimension. I base this largely on ET's theology, which will be discussed later.

I believe that demons—masquerading as aliens—are taking individuals on a journey against their will in order to indoctrinate them. In essence, the abduction is real—I just don't know how much of it is physical rather than psychological or spiritual. Abductees could be taken on board a real, physical UFO craft, or it could be some sort of a mental projection or charade induced by the demonic entities involved. It is all "real" to the abductee, and there are often physical marks and scars after these abduction events, so some aspect of it is physical. Alien abductions are a spiritual event taking place in a physical environment, and I don't have enough information to neatly separate the physical from the spiritual aspects. UFOs are real, and abductions are UFO-associated phenomena. Regardless of where the line is drawn between the physical and spiritual aspects of UFOs and abductions, the important point to keep in mind is that we are dealing with ongoing supernatural deception.

While abductees are convinced that they are abducted in their physical body and have physical injuries to prove it, a good case can be made that the abduction is an out-of-body experience. Abductees often report that they are transported through a wall or ceiling during the abduction. As clever and deceptive as ET is, I would think transporting an abductee's physical body through a wall or closed window is problematic. An out-of-body or spiritual abduction is an alternate consideration. Individuals undergoing a near-death experience (NDE) often describe themselves as leaving their physical body and passing through walls and ceilings while completely aware of their surroundings.[7] While NDEs are an entirely different experience from alien abductions, the out-of-body aspects of NDEs have some common ground with abduction experiences.

We know from Scripture that Satan is an amazingly powerful entity capable of impressive signs and wonders which will be displayed during the end time. UFOs and abductions are examples of his deceptive powers in our present age. Perhaps ET has the ability to transport himself and a physical body through a wall. As I pointed out earlier, all matter, including human beings and what we consider a solid wall, is mostly empty space. Perhaps ET is deceptive enough to convince an abductee that they have passed through a wall or closed window. UFOs don't obey our understanding of physics, so I don't imagine ET is obliged to or limited to our understanding of physics. I won't try to resolve the physical/spiritual aspects of alien abductions. However, the issue of greater importance is the perceived reality of the abduction and the real identity of ET. My objective is to unmask ET and reveal his deceptions and, to the extent possible, his intentions.

Many abductees suffer from physical ailments and are troubled by an experience they can't fully explain or remember after their abduction event. Apart from abductions, there's a history of physical and psychological trauma among individuals having a close encounter with a UFO. Headaches and nightmares are commonly reported by abductees. Some abductees have some conscious memory of parts of the abduction experience or viewing a UFO, but most of the experience seems buried in their subconscious mind. Details of the abduction experience come to consciousness during hypnotic regression, and the abductee tends to relive the experience in detail with associated emotional and physical reactions.

While abductees report that they are wide-awake during the bulk of the abduction experience, it seems that, after the fact, the experience is largely embedded in their subconscious. This subconscious memory of an abduction experience seems, in some cases, to manifest as emotional or even physical distress, but the bulk of the details of the event typically only come to the conscious mind through hypnotic regression. Abductees are often told by the alien abductors that they will not remember the experience, or they are told to forget it. I suspect the abduction experience may be experienced in an altered state of consciousness—perhaps something like demonic possession—and comes to light or conscious memory when the individual is put into a similar altered state of consciousness induced by hypnosis.

Who Are the Abductees?

Before we look at the abduction experience in some detail, it's important to have an idea of who is being abducted by aliens. It turns out that individuals reporting abductions are, by any standard, normal people from various walks of life. Working class people, professionals, housewives, and people from many different ethnicities have been subjects of the abduction experience. The experience itself often leaves troubling emotional scars and sometimes physical scars, but researchers say the people reporting alien abductions do not appear to be unique.

Alien abductions are often not one-time events. It is often discovered that the abductions begin at an early age, as young as ages three to five years. The interaction an abductee has with abducting aliens is age-related. Children encounter alien playmates, and adults receive serious information and instructions. The abductions appear to be an acclimation and indoctrination process.

Sometimes alien-abduction experiences occur in more than one family member and sometimes in more than one family generation. Abductions usually occur with one individual at a time, but sometimes two people are abducted at once.

Are you, the reader, subject to an alien abduction? Have you experienced or do you suspect you have experienced an abduction? Have you had a close encounter with a UFO or what you believe to be an alien entity? Are you fearful of an alien abduction or encounter? If you have already had an encounter or abduction, do you fear a repeat? If you have any of these concerns or fears, read on to chapter eight. There is a way to be alien- and abduction-proof and free of fear; find out how in chapter eight. But first, let's look at a typical alien abduction in the next chapter.

CHAPTER 7

The Abduction Experience

What is it like? What happens when someone is "abducted" by aliens? In this chapter we will take a close look at what happens when an individual is abducted by aliens. This will be a distillation of accounts described on the internet, in TV interviews, and in the books recommended in the introduction to this book.

Not every abduction is exactly like all others, but there are similarities or commonalities that have allowed researchers to develop what they call the Classic Abduction Syndrome (CAS). Our description will follow the lines of a CAS.

The Abduction

Every abduction begins with an individual being captured and abducted against their will. Sometimes two people are abducted together, but more often it involves just one person. The abduction can take place day or night and in most any place, but most often it occurs at night when a person is in bed or sometimes while driving a car.

If a person is driving a car when the abduction occurs, they typically first see a UFO, which eventually approaches them. They may stop the car, or often the car engine dies. The failure of electronic and electromechanical devices often occurs in the presence of a UFO. Aircraft often report system failures, or a car engine and lights may fail. The abductee may or may not recall being taken from the car and into a spacecraft by aliens. The details of the abduction are usually made manifest during a subsequent hypnotic regression. After the abduction, the individual typically has no recollection of the abduction but finds themselves in the car miles down the road from where they last remembered being. This is accompanied by up to an hour or more of missing time. Missing time is a common element of a CAS.

More often the abduction occurs during the night when the abductee is in bed. The individual may sense the presence of an entity, or bright lights may penetrate the bedroom from outside. Some abductees report a humming sound or vibrations. The alien entities may enter the bedroom through closed windows, a wall, or the ceiling. The abductee finds they are paralyzed and unable to move. They are terrified and outraged, wanting to scream or call for help, but they are unable. If there is a spouse or other person in bed with the abductee, they appear as if in a trance, not perceiving the aliens or the abduction.

The abductees are levitated above the bed and escorted—often in a horizontal position—by aliens as they pass through a wall, window, or the ceiling to a waiting UFO. Often the abductee feels they are levitated and transported by a beam of light from the UFO. Abductees have reported that they can see their house and other buildings below them as they are levitated to the UFO.

The aliens participating in the abduction are described in various ways, but the most common description is of what is known as a "gray." A gray is usually a short entity with gray- or light-colored skin. They have a thin body and limbs and a large head which appears out of proportion compared to the body. The head is somewhat triangular, being larger at the top than at the bottom. The grays have very large, out-of-proportion eyes that taper at the inner and outer edges. The eyes are typically black with no noticeable whites or pupils. Their nose is not much more than a bump with two small holes, and the mouth is a small, thin slit without significant lips.

The Examination

Abductees are typically escorted and floated into a waiting UFO through an opening in the bottom or side of the craft. If the UFO is on the ground, there is usually a ramp to an opening. Once inside, the abductee finds themselves in a room with curved walls. The light in the room sometimes appears to come from the walls. Different alien types are often seen going about various tasks or working with what appear to be electronic equipment or systems along the walls. The abductee is placed on a table and a terrifying, abusive, intrusive, painful, humiliating "medical" examination follows.

The abductee is often stripped naked for the "medical" examination. I call it a medical examination, but what follows seems bizarre, brutal, and primitive by any reasonable standard. During the examination, probes are typically inserted into every bodily orifice, and needles and probes are inserted into the body through the skin in various locations. Often skin and bodily fluid samples are taken. Sperm is often extracted from male abductees, and eggs are harvested from female abductees.

The entity doing the "medical" procedures is often referred to as the "doctor" by abductees. Sometimes the "doctor" is perceived to be a female. The "doctor" entity is taller than the grays, with light skin, sometimes with wrinkles, and appears to be an authority among the other attending aliens.

During abduction encounters the aliens usually communicate with abductees mind-to-mind or telepathically rather than with verbal speech. When an abductee expresses fear or rage over the abduction or "medical" procedures, the aliens seem oblivious or advise them that they won't remember the experience and that it's all "necessary." Abductees often report they feel like they are being treated like animals by the aliens who are examining them. Sometimes the aliens appear to do something that calms the abductee and reduces the pain involved in the procedures. Abductees often resist looking directly into the eyes of the aliens, as they feel the eyes are controlling and through them the alien can see or know everything about them.

Abductees often report that they believe the aliens have implanted a tracking device in their body during the "medical" examination. After an abduction experience, some abductees have had objects removed from under their skin that they believe were alien tracking implants. When examined, these objects appear to have a keratin shell. Keratin is a hard protein found in fingernails but wouldn't normally be found in other locations under the skin. Under the keratin shell, something metallic has been reported, and under extreme magnification, microtubules have been observed. The objects are hard to explain, but no evidence of how it could be a tracking device has been presented.

The fact that alien abductions are often not a one-time event seems to reinforce the idea of tracking abductees. During hypnotic regression, abductees often report repeated abductions since childhood. This revelation, under hypnosis, often seems to explain childhood or previous dreams that have troubled the abductee for years.

The Alien-Human Hybrid Program

During the "medical" examination, I reported that sperm is often extracted from male abductees and eggs from females. Add to this the fact that abductees are sometimes induced to have sex with an alien. Female abductees have claimed to have become pregnant by sex with an alien or by or a fertilization process during an abduction. They then report that an alien-human hybrid fetus was removed from them during a subsequent abduction.

Both male and female abductees have reported being shown large numbers of alien-human hybrid fetuses being maintained in liquid-filled glass containers aboard the UFO. Some are shown alien-human hybrid children and encouraged to play with them. Sometimes abductees are told that one or more of the alien-human hybrids are their own offspring from previous abduction experiences.

Abductees are told various things about the purpose of the alien-human hybrid program. Some are told that the hybrids are an evolutionary process to incorporate the best of both alien and human attributes in a new race. The alien-human hybrids will populate other planets or repopulate the earth after a coming worldwide cataclysm described below. Some abductees are told that aliens have evolved spiritually and intellectually beyond humans, but they have lost the emotional capabilities that humans possess. Humans have the ability to feel positive emotions like pleasure and love, but we also have negative or bad emotions, like anger and hate, which aliens don't possess. Supposedly, the alien-human hybrids will retain the intellectual and spiritual attributes of the aliens and gain the ability to feel love and positive emotions as humans without the bad emotions like hate, fear, and anger.

UFOs are an unconventional and strange phenomenon. UFO-associated aliens and abductions add "weird" to unconventional and strange and an alien-human hybrid program adds "bizarre" to the list. However, if we remember to think of the aliens not as extraterrestrial visitors but as deceiving demonic fallen angels as described in previous chapters, we may be able to see a plan behind the bizarre. We are using God's Word, the Bible, as the absolute standard of truth, so let's look at this from a scriptural perspective.

I should point out that the following explanation for the alien-human hybrid program is not universally accepted among Christians. Nevertheless, it is a position held by some biblical scholars. The book titled *Alien Encounters* by Missler and Eastman (recommended in the introduction) gives a detailed description of this position, and I recommend it for careful consideration.

In Genesis 6:1–4, during the days just before the flood, the Bible says that the "sons of God" took wives from the "daughters of men" and produced exceptional offspring called "Nephilim" who were "mighty men" and "men of renown." Here are the verses in the English Standard Bible:

When man began to multiply on the face of the land and daughters were born to them, the sons of God saw that the daughters of man were attractive. And they took as their wives any they chose. Then the LORD said, "My Spirit shall not abide in man forever, for he is flesh: his days shall be 120 years." The Nephilim were on the earth in those days, and also afterward, when the sons of God came in to the daughters of man and they bore children to them. These were the mighty men who were of old, the men of renown.

Scholars debate over exactly what these verses are describing, but most agree that the term "sons of God" in the Old Testament refers to angels. The Good News Bible, in plain English, uses the term "heavenly beings" in place of "sons of God." Virtually all scholars agree that the term "daughters of men" refers to female humans. The union of angels and human women were exceptional beings (mighty and renowned) called Nephilim.

Biblical scholars have interpreted these verses in various ways, but some scholars maintain that a straightforward interpretation of these verses describes angels, specifically fallen angels or demons, having intercourse with female humans and producing hybrid entities called Nephilim.

The propagation of Nephilim into the human population described here is in the time just preceding the flood that destroyed almost all life except the family of Noah and animals on the ark. Noah is described in Genesis 6:9 (KJV) as "a just man and perfect in his generations, and Noah walked with God." The expression "perfect in his generations" can be interpreted to mean that Noah's family was not contaminated with the Nephilim strain. All of the Nephilim described in the time of Noah were wiped out by the flood, and the earthly population proceeded uncontaminated thereafter.

Unfortunately, the flood was not a permanent fix for the Nephilim problem. Genesis 6:4 (above) says, "The Nephilim were on the earth in those days, **and also afterward....**" So the problem of fallen angels mating with humans did not go away; it occurred again. In Numbers 13:33 when the Israelites sent scouts to survey the promised land, some reported, "We saw the Nephilim (the sons of Anak, who come from the Nephilim), and we seemed to ourselves like grasshoppers, and so we seemed to them."

Bear in mind that within our biblical worldview, the human race is in the midst of a huge spiritual battle (Ephesians 6:12) between Satan with his fellow fallen angels and God. Satan and his fallen angels (demons) were highly motivated to corrupt the line of the promised Savior, so contaminating the human population with Nephilim may well have been a tactic.

If this interpretation of Scripture is accurate, then fallen (demonic) angels and humans have been and possibly are continuing to procreate with humans as described in alien abductions. Accordingly, the alien-human hybrid project could be an extension of a Satanic plan. In Matthew 24:38–39, Jesus is describing his second coming, and he said conditions on earth will be like "those days before the flood...until the day when Noah entered the ark." From Genesis 6:1–4, we know that fallen angel-demons were procreating with humans, and Nephilim were on the earth during the days before the flood. Based on this, some biblical scholars believe that Nephilim will play a role in end-time events, and the alien abduction and alien-human hybrid program is setting the stage for the biblical end times.

The Alien's Purpose and Theology

After the "medical" examination and procedures, abductees may be given a tour of the UFO and introduced to various aliens, alien-human hybrids, or other humans. Some abductees claim to have met Jesus, a pope, or other religious figures on board a UFO. The aliens portray themselves as highly advanced technologically and spiritually and claim they are here to help the human race progress to a higher level of spiritual consciousness.

The aliens have told abductees that they are from a distant planet or star system. Years ago, they told abductees they were from Mars or Venus or someplace in our solar system, but our science has determined these planets aren't habitable;

they have reported that they are from other distant locations. They frequently claim to be from the Andromeda galaxy or the Pleiades star systems.

While on board the UFO, abductees are often told about or shown videos of a future catastrophic destruction of the earth through war resulting from man's hate and propensity for violence or particularly from ecological disaster resulting from our shameful ecological abuse of the earth. Sometimes abductees are told that the future disaster is unavoidable; others are told they have been chosen to help prevent the future catastrophe by teaching others to love and care for others and our planet.

Essentially, demons—disguised as ET—are telling abductees that humans are a mess and messing up the earth and disrupting the cosmic consciousness shared by them and various alien entities throughout the universe. Their goal is to help humans advance to a higher level of spiritual consciousness and thus join in harmony with the cosmic consciousness that connects mind and matter throughout the universe. Abductees are told that man's concept of God and various religions are man's attempt to understand the universal cosmic consciousness.

The theology of aliens is recognizable as variations of traditional Eastern mysticism and New Age theology. The pantheistic concept of the continuum or conflation of mind and matter is prominent. Other theological concepts promoted by aliens include reincarnation, spiritual advancement, connection with the cosmic consciousness, channeling with other spiritual beings, out-of-body experiences, and astral travel. Some abductees come to "remember" previous lives, and some believe they are actually aliens in a human body on a mission to earth. These individuals see the UFO or another planet as their real home and long to return "home." When undergoing hypnotic regression, some abductees who believe they are aliens in human bodies, or an alien-human hybrid, will speak in the first person as the alien rather than the human.

Aftereffects of the Abduction Experience

The abduction experience is ended when the abductee is returned to their bed or car, usually where the experience began. The abductee may have some recollection of the experience but more often will have no particular conscious recollection of the abduction. Nevertheless, the abduction experience does have aftereffects.

While the abductee may have some recollection of seeing a UFO or aliens, it is unusual for the abductee to remember much of the abduction experience apart from hypnotic regression. The abductee may have marks and bruises on their body that they can't explain and a troubling feeling that something has happened that they can't recall. Some abductees have head-aches, nosebleeds, or bad dreams following an abduction. Even if the abductee can't recall details of the abduction experience, they know or feel something has happened, and they may fear the return of alien entities when in bed at night. The bad dreams and partial memories may be so troubling for some abductees that they seek professional help.

When an abductee finds or is referred to a psychologist or professional familiar with the alien-abduction syndrome, they often seek to understand the experience through hypnotic regression. When the experience is brought from the subconscious to the conscious mind, the abductee is typically amazed by what he or she learns. They struggle to understand and fit what they learn through hypnotic regression with their sense of reality. They may question their own sanity for a time. Some abductees will seek spiritual counseling, but few pastors are familiar with the abduction experience and able to offer assistance beyond referring them to psychiatric help.

Abductees often find or are referred to group therapy with others who are wrestling with similar experiences and issues. In these group sessions, abductees are grateful to find that they are not alone and that others have had similar experiences.

After their abduction experiences, some abductees become involved with ecology or environmental causes, organizations, or issues. Some develop psychic or healing interests and abilities. Others become involved in New Age (alien) theology, and some continue to communicate with alien entities through channeling or visitations.

I should point out that some abductees experience what they call a breakthrough in which they come to believe that the alien abductors are well intentioned with mankind's best interests in mind. These individuals even feel love for the aliens and feel it is returned by the aliens. This breakthrough is achieved by getting beyond the fear they feel with the abduction experience. Given the frightening, humiliating, painful "medical" examination that abductees often experience, I can't help but associate this breakthrough from fear to love as something like the Stockholm syndrome. With the Stockholm syndrome, a kidnapping victim held as a hostage begins to identify, bond with, and trust their captors despite the power imbalance and abusive treatment. It's a psychological "safe place," or attempt to mitigate a threat by turning an enemy into a "friend."

ET's Theology from a Biblical Perspective

When we compare ET's theology to biblical theology, we can clearly see that he is not the spiritually advanced extraterrestrial he claims to be. The Bible is the Word of God, the Creator of the universe, and the standard by which to measure all things, including ET and his theology. ET is a deceiving spiritual entity denying and defying the biblical God of all creation with a false message and gospel. ET is portraying himself as a spiritually enlightened being, offering a path to spiritual advancement to a pitiful and corrupt human race. We are warned in 2 Corinthians 11:14–15 that "even Satan disguises himself as an angel of light. So it is no surprise if his servants, also, disguise themselves as servants of righteousness." How does one distinguish the good guys from the bad guys in the ongoing spiritual battle described in Ephesians 6:12? By the Word of God, the Bible. In John 14:6, Jesus said, "'I am the way, and the truth, and the life. No one comes to the Father except through me.'" If you want to know the truth, don't listen to ET—listen to Jesus; He is the truth personified.

ET comes in amazing UFO vehicles and claims to be a technologically and spiritually evolved life form visiting from a distant planet. This is a lie. ET's claim to be an evolved life form from another planet intentionally contradicts the fact that God is the Creator of all things, including all life. ET didn't evolve on another planet. Life didn't evolve on earth either—it was created by God. ET is a created spiritual being that rebelled against his Creator and was cast out of Heaven. ET is a fallen angel—a demon—in league with a powerful fallen angel called Lucifer, or Satan. The objective or mission of Satan and his fallen-angel cohorts—sometimes posing as ET—is to oppose God and deceive and lead the human race, who is created in the image of God, away from God and His plan of salvation.

We humans should not be swayed by amazing signs and wonders such as ET and his amazing UFO vehicles. Our anchor to truth is the Word of God, not signs and wonders. Scripture tells us in Luke 21:11 that as the end time approaches there will be deceptive "terrors and great signs from heaven." First Timothy 4:1 warns us, "In later times some will depart from the faith by devoting themselves to deceitful spirits and teachings of demons."

ET's theology ("teachings of demons") offers mankind spiritual enlightenment or advancement, but he offers no salvation. ET is partly correct when he portrays mankind as violent, hateful, and corrupt. Human history affirms this without ET's input. According to Scripture, mankind is fallen; we are all sinful creatures falling short of God's standards (Romans 3:23). The Bible tells us that we are all sinners, and the wages of sin is death. Accordingly, we all face death (Romans 6:23), so we all stand in need of salvation. God offers us salvation free of charge by placing our faith in Jesus Christ, who died on the cross in our place (Romans 5:8) to pay for our sins if we receive his forgiveness through faith. In John 14:6 quoted above, Jesus said He is the "way," the "truth," and the "life," and "no one comes to the Father except through me." Jesus is not "a" way to salvation, he is "the" way to salvation. As Acts 4:12 puts it,

"There is salvation in no one else, for there is no other name under heaven given among men by which we must be saved."

ET's theology offers no remedy for man's sin and no salvation. Followers of ET's theology are following doctrines of demons (I Timothy 4:1), not the Word of God. ET's followers may see signs and wonders and communicate with what they believe are enlightened spiritual beings, but they are being deceived and led away from the truth of Scripture. ET offers spiritual advancement and reincarnation in place of salvation, but the Bible refutes reincarnation in Hebrews 9:27 (KJV) when it says, "It is appointed unto men once to die, but after this the judgment." With a sure judgment coming and eternity in the balance, will you put your faith in ET's "spiritual enlightenment" or the free salvation of Jesus Christ who died on the cross for your sins? Choose wisely.

CHAPTER 8

The Biblical Answer to the UFO Deception

In previous chapters we have identified the "unidentified" element of UFOs and associated ETs. We don't know everything about UFOs and ET, but we know *who* ET is. When we examine UFOs and so-called extraterrestrial aliens through the framework of biblical authority, their identity is clear. The entities masquerading as extraterrestrial aliens are Satanic demons with impressive UFO technology for window dressing to give ET the appearance of authority and credibility by virtue of advanced technological knowhow. UFOs and associated ETs are a manifestation of the age-old spiritual warfare described in Scripture. Specifically, the UFO/ET phenomenon is an aspect of the ongoing Satanic attempt to distract and confuse mankind and point him away from scriptural truth and the God of the Bible who is mankind's only hope for salvation.

We have identified UFOs and associated ETs as Satanic based on their theology, which has been conveyed to many thousands of abductees and contactees around the world. Their theology contradicts the absolute truth of Scripture found in the

Bible. God's Word is truth, and when we hold ETs theology up to the truth of Scripture, ET is shown to be a liar and deceiver. We know from Scripture that Satan is a liar and deceiver (John 8:44). We also know from Scripture that Satan and his demons can appear as angels of light and servants of righteousness (2 Corinthians 11:14–15), so appearing as helpful extraterrestrial aliens is consistent with Satan's deceptive character.

UFOs and their associated ET entities are not extraterrestrial in the sense that they come from another planet or galaxy. They are extraterrestrial because they come and go from another dimension—a spiritual dimension. More accurately, we should say that UFOs and associated entities are extradimensional. Scripture gives us examples of angels and demons coming into and exiting from our familiar earthly physical environment. UFOs and associated entities come into and exit our earthly dimension from a spiritual dimension just as angels and demons are demonstrated to do in Scripture.

Interestingly, the intrusion of Satanic demons into our dimensional universe is not new. The portraying of themselves as extraterrestrial aliens is fairly new, but in the past, they have manifested in forms that conform to cultural expectations. Tales of ghosts, fairies, and goblins fill historic literature. Perhaps the ancient gods and characters of Greek and Roman theology were demonic intrusions into history. These ancient goblins and "gods" were sometimes reported to seduce humans producing demigod offspring. Perhaps demigods are what Scripture refers to as Nephilim. Demonic entities masquerading as ET are a contemporary manifestation of the age-old spiritual battle. With an evolutionary worldview and human technology knocking on the doors of outer space, our culture is primed for ET's deceptions and ready for—perhaps even anticipating—the arrival of ET from the far reaches of our universe.

How do Satan and the demons make UFOs come into our earthly environment and perform the amazing feats they do? We don't know how, but we do know that Satan is a powerful entity and will perform spectacular supernatural phenomena to deceive mankind in the end times. In many UFO reports I have read, the UFOs appear to perform unusual or even bizarre movements in the sky, often displaying various colored lights as if trying to attract attention. UFOs also come in strange shapes other than saucers and orbs. I have wondered if such behavior and strange shapes are an attempt to be seen and noticed to build a repertoire of UFO "believers" in preparation for a future revelation and deception.

The book of Revelation records many Satanic supernatural events during the end times. We know that in the end times "there will be terrors and great signs from heaven" (Luke 21:11). Matthew 24:24 tells us that during the end times there will be "false prophets" who will perform "great signs and wonders" that will be exceptionally deceptive. One wonders if this might include UFOs and lying aliens with their bag of tricks.

Born Again Christians Need Not Fear ET or Abduction

An interesting fact is reported by UFO and alien-abduction researchers. While many thousands of people from a wide variety of backgrounds have reported abductions and encounters with alien ETs, no Bible-believing Christians have reported being abducted against their will. In addition to this, when an abductee invokes the name of Jesus Christ, the demons masquerading as ET leave them alone. This is yet another indication of who ET is. In Luke 10:17 when Jesus sent some of his disciples on a mission, they returned saying, "Lord, even the demons are subject to us in your name!" James 4:7 (NASB) says, "Submit therefore to God. But resist the devil, and he will flee from you."

The key to victory over Satan and his demons—whether disguised as extraterrestrial aliens, ghosts, goblins, or angels of light—is Jesus Christ. Scripture is full of examples where Jesus and His disciples cast demons out of possessed individuals. Individuals, including Christians, have no power over Satan and his demons, but Jesus Christ does. Christians who have placed their faith in and are "in Christ" can call on the authority of their Savior to protect them from Satanic entities. A true Christian need not fear alien abduction, as any

Satanic encounter can be ended by calling on Christ, our God and Savior.

As a point of caution, I would say that I don't think the name "Jesus Christ" is a magic word or phrase that anyone can use to defeat demons. It is true that the name Jesus Christ is a powerful name, and according to Philippians 2:10–11, one day every knee in heaven and earth "and under the earth" will bow "and every tongue confess that Jesus Christ is Lord." Even the most powerful demonic entities are subject to Jesus Christ. According to Matthew 7:21–23, it appears that even nonbelievers can, on occasion, cast out demons in Christ's name. However, the only safe position from which to withstand or confront a demonic entity is from a personal relationship with Christ. A true believer who has, by faith, received Jesus Christ as his or her Savior and is indwelt by the Holy Spirit can call on the Lord Jesus Christ for protection against Satan and his demons. God protects His own, but I don't know that a secularist (non-believer) can always use the words "Jesus Christ" as a magical phrase to defeat a Satanic threat. The power is in the person of Christ, not the words. The ultimate protection is to be in a personal relationship with Christ, which entitles you to call on His power and authority for protection.

Trust Scripture, Not Signs and Wonders

When the Israelites were about to enter the promised land, God warned them through Moses not to be led astray by individuals with false messages, even if accompanied by signs and wonders. This is described as follows in Deuteronomy 13:1–3:

> If a prophet or a dreamer of dreams arises among you and gives you a sign or a wonder, and the sign or wonder that he tells you comes to pass, and if he says, "Let us go after other gods," which you have not known, "and let us serve them," you shall not listen to the words of that prophet or that dreamer of dreams. For the LORD your God is testing you, to know whether you love the LORD your God with all your heart and with all your soul.

In a sense, today we are living in a time of testing. UFOs are frequently in the news, and UFO-associated entities are proclaiming a theology that contradicts the Word of God. It turns out that millions of people around the world believe they have been abducted by aliens, and thousands more are buying into ET's New Age theology and proactively seeking contact and guidance from what they believe are extraterrestrial aliens. An internet search will reveal no shortage of people around the world who believe they are or have been in touch with and/or abducted by extraterrestrial aliens. Some are channeling aliens, writing books, or making videos explaining their encounters and spreading ET's new-age theology. A CBS survey found that two-thirds of the United States population already believe in the existence of extraterrestrial intelligent life. A survey reported by *Newsweek* on June 8, 2021, found that 43 percent of the US population is more interested in UFOs and aliens since the recent release of military UFO videos.[8] What would it take for these people to believe in ET's theology? What sort of miracles or signs and wonders do you think the demonic entities have in store for humanity? Will alien bodies be recovered at a UFO crash site? Will aliens make a public appearance? The existence of UFOs alone is enough for many to seek communication with them. I suspect millions of people with no foundation or faith in biblical truth would be swayed toward ET's theology on the basis of his signs and wonders.

ET's UFOs are lying signs and wonders—window dress-ing— to capture the imagination of mankind and convince us that they are technologically and intellectually advanced so that we might believe them when they claim to be spiritu-ally advanced and here to help us join them in their theology. Ephesians 2:1–2 seems to hint at this when it refers to the fatal flaw of following the doctrines of Satan, who is referred to as the prince of the "power of the air" or "space" as the Good News Translation puts it. ET's doctrine substitutes lies for the truth of Scripture, and this identifies him as a Satanic being—an enemy of God.

When we hold ET's words and theology up to the light of biblical authority, we can clearly see who ET is. ET says he is here to enlighten mankind and bring us to a higher level of spiritual consciousness, but the Bible tells us that "even Satan disguises himself as an angel of light. So it is no surprise if his servants, also, disguise themselves as servants of righteousness. Their end will correspond to their deeds" (2 Corinthians 11:14–15). Paul warns us in Galatians 1:8, "If we or an angel from heaven should preach to you a gospel contrary to the one we preached to you, let him be accursed."

We must not forget Jesus's description of Satan in John 8:44 when he challenges those opposing his ministry:

> You are of your father the devil, and your will is to do your father's desires. He was a murderer from the beginning, and does not stand in the truth, because there is no truth in him. When he lies, he speaks out of his own character, for he is a liar and the father of lies. (John 8:44)

When the evidence is considered, it is clear that UFOs and associated ETs are a manifestation of spiritual warfare that began with the fall of Satan and first impacted mankind in Genesis chapter 3. Paul, in Ephesians 6:12, reminds us that "we do not wrestle against flesh and blood, but against the rulers, against the authorities, against the cosmic powers over this present darkness, against the spiritual forces of evil in the heavenly places." UFOs and ET are entering our world from a spiritual dimension to deceive mankind and direct us away from the God of the Bible and his plan of salvation found only by faith in Christ. In place of salvation, ET offers his version of spiritual enlightenment—a fatal lie. The UFOs seen in our worldly environment are props—signs and wonders intended to lend credibility to the message of demons in ET costumes.

As already noted, I am inclined to think the UFO/alien deception may play a significant role in end-time events. I was surprised to learn that there are many individuals and organizations around the world using meditation to communicate with what they believe are UFO-associated entities and spiritual guides. Often these groups claim to see appearances of UFOs and/or aliens during their sessions. Such signs and wonders are used to "set the hook" in order to reel the uninformed into the deception.

It's important to realize that UFOs and alien abductions are not the whole of spiritual warfare—they are just a prominent front in the battle. There are many spiritual pathways leading away from scriptural truth. If you remove the UFOs and aliens, you will still find people around the world meditating to communicate with "spirits" or connect to a cosmic consciousness. Spiritualism, the idea that a person or medium can communicate with spirits or the dead, has been around for centuries . . . just like UFOs. Attempting to communicate with any spiritual identity apart from the one true God of the Bible is extremely dangerous. Whether masquerading as an ascended master, an extraterrestrial, or dearly departed Aunt Bessy, there is no shortage of ways to deceive one seeking truth or spiritual connection apart from the one true God revealed in the Bible.

The Christian responsibility in the matter of the UFO/ET phenomenon is to be informed and understand the world and times we are living in. It would be a mistake for Christians to ignore or underestimate the impact of the UFO phenomenon on the secular culture and on ill-informed Christians. Christians must be grounded in Scripture in order to know the truth of God's Word and to recognize the deception, lies, and false theology of ET. Christians must trust God's Word over lying stories even if accompanied by signs and wonders. Christians must counter the false gospel of ET with warnings, the truth of Scripture, and God's offer of salvation by faith in Jesus Christ, "for there is no other name under heaven given among men by which we must be saved" (Acts 4:12).

The following, final chapter is a scriptural resource to help the reader know the truth in order to recognize the lies that are part of the UFO deception. If you read or are told any spiritual message or theological doctrine that contradicts the Word of God as found in the Bible, you can know that it is a deception.

A Final Word and a Warning

In this work I have talked a lot about so-called alien abductions, but I must point out that there are other terrifying spiritual and physically dangerous hazards connected with UFOs and associated phenomena. The book *Skinwalkers in the Pentagon*, listed in the introduction, documents many frightening spiritual encounters and potentially fatal diseases resulting from close encounters with UFOs and related paranormal phenomena. I caution the reader to NEVER seek a UFO or alien encounter and NEVER approach or interact with a UFO if the opportunity presents itself.

Don't fear or become obsessed with UFOs. Instead, fear and become obsessed with the God of the Bible who either is or can be your eternal Savior. Proverbs 1:7 tells us, "The fear of the LORD is the beginning of knowledge." No human is a match for the power of the least of demonic entities, but no demonic entity is a match for the God of the Bible. If you, by faith, have received Jesus Christ into your life as Lord and Savior, then God's Holy Spirit dwells within you, and as 1 John 4:4 puts it, "He who is in you is greater than he who is in the world." Being "in Christ" is the only safe place in a fallen and dangerous world.

CHAPTER 9

Bible Verses Relevant to the UFO Deception

The following Bible verses are provided to facilitate a scriptural assessment of the UFO and associated phenomena. God's Word is the ultimate and universal truth and light by which to live our lives and evaluate all things.

God Is the Creator of Everything, and Man Was Created in His Image

Genesis 1:1: "In the beginning, God created the heavens and the earth."

Genesis 1:14–18: "And God said, 'Let there be lights in the expanse of the heavens to separate the day from the night. And let them be for signs and for seasons, and for days and years, and let them be lights in the expanse of the heavens to give light upon the earth.' And it was so. And God made the two great lights—the greater light to rule the day and the lesser light to rule the night—and the stars. And God set them in the expanse of the heavens to give light on the earth, to rule over the day and over the night, and to separate the light from the darkness. And God saw that it was good."

Genesis 1:26–28: "Then God said, 'Let us make man in our image, after our likeness. And let them have dominion over the fish of the sea and over the birds of the heavens and over the livestock and over all the earth and over every creeping thing that creeps on the earth.' So God created man in his own image, in the image of God he created him; male and female he created them. And God blessed them. And God said to them, 'Be fruitful and multiply and fill the earth and subdue it, and have dominion over the fish of the sea and over the birds of the heavens and over every living thing that moves on the earth.'"

Genesis 1:31: "And God saw everything that he had made, and behold, it was very good. And there was evening and there was morning, the sixth day."

Genesis 2:1–2: "Thus the heavens and the earth were finished, and all the host of them. And on the seventh day God finished his work that he had done, and he rested on the seventh day from all his work that he had done."

Isaiah 45:18: "For thus says the LORD, who created the heavens (he is God!), who formed the earth and made it (he established it; he did not create it empty, he formed it to be inhabited!): 'I am the LORD, and there is no other.'"

Jesus Is God and Is Involved in the Creation of Everything

Matthew 1:23 (KJV): "Behold, a virgin shall be with child, and shall bring forth a son, and they shall call his name Emmanuel, which being interpreted is, God with us."

John 1:1–3: "In the beginning was the Word, and the Word was with God, and the Word was God. He was in the beginning with God. All things were made through him, and without him was not anything made that was made."

John 1:10: "He was in the world, and the world was made through him, yet the world did not know him."

John 8:58 (KJV): "Jesus said unto them, Verily, verily, I say unto you, Before Abraham was, I am."

Colossians 1:15–17: "He is the image of the invisible God, the firstborn of all creation. For by him all things were created, in heaven and on earth, visible and invisible, whether thrones or dominions or rulers or authorities—all things were created through him and for him. And he is before all things, and in him all things hold together."

The Fall of Man and Nature

Genesis 2:16–17: "And the LORD God commanded the man, saying, 'You may surely eat of every tree of the garden, but of the tree of the knowledge of good and evil you shall not eat, for in the day that you eat of it you shall surely die.'"

Genesis 3:4–6 (GNT): "The snake replied, 'That's not true; you will not die. God said that because he knows that when you eat it, you will be like God and know what is good and what is bad.' The woman saw how beautiful the tree was and how good its fruit would be to eat, and she thought how wonderful it would be to become wise. So she took some of the fruit and ate it. Then she gave some to her husband, and he also ate it."

Genesis 3:17–19: "And to Adam he said, 'Because you have listened to the voice of your wife and have eaten of the tree of which I commanded you, "You shall not eat of it," cursed is the ground because of you; in pain you shall eat of it all the days of your life; thorns and thistles it shall bring forth for you; and you shall eat the plants of the field. By the sweat of your face you shall eat bread, till you return to the ground, for out of it you were taken; for you are dust, and to dust you shall return.'"

1 Corinthians 15:21–22: "For as by a man came death, by a man has come also the resurrection of the dead. For as in Adam all die, so also in Christ shall all be made alive."

1 Corinthians 15:26: "The last enemy to be destroyed is death."

Romans 5:12 (KJV): "Wherefore, as by one man sin entered into the world, and death by sin; and so death passed upon all men, for that all have sinned."

Romans 6:23: "For the wages of sin is death, but the free gift of God is eternal life in Christ Jesus our Lord."

Romans 8:20–22: "For the creation was subjected to futility, not willingly, but because of him who subjected it, in hope that the creation itself will be set free from its bondage to corruption and obtain the freedom of the glory of the children of God. For we know that the whole creation has been groaning together in the pains of childbirth until now."

God's Plan of Salvation through Faith in Christ Alone

Isaiah 53:1–12 (GNT): "The people reply, 'Who would have believed what we now report? Who could have seen the LORD's hand in this? It was the will of the LORD that his servant grow like a plant taking root in dry ground. He had no dignity or beauty to make us take notice of him. There was nothing attractive about him, nothing that would draw us to him. We despised him and rejected him; he endured suffering and pain. No one would even look at him—we ignored him as if he were nothing. But he endured the suffering that should have been ours, the pain that we should have borne. All the while we thought that his suffering was punishment sent by God. But because of our sins he was wounded, beaten because of the evil we did. We are healed by the punishment he suffered, made whole by the blows he received. All of us were like sheep that were lost, each of us going his own way. But the LORD made the punishment fall on him, the punishment all of us deserved. He was treated harshly, but endured it humbly; he never said a word. Like a lamb about to be slaughtered, like a sheep about to be sheared, he never said a word. He was arrested and sentenced and led off to die, and no one cared about his fate. He was put to death for the sins of our people. He was placed in a grave with those who are evil, he was buried with the rich, even though he had never committed a crime or ever told a lie.' The LORD says, 'It was my will that he should suffer; his death was a sacrifice to bring forgiveness. And so he will see his descendants; he will live a long life, and through him my purpose will succeed. After a life of suffering, he will again have joy; he will know that he did not suffer in vain. My devoted servant, with whom I am pleased, will bear the punishment of many and for his sake

I will forgive them. And so I will give him a place of honor, a place among the great and powerful. He willingly gave his life and shared the fate of evil men. He took the place of many sinners and prayed that they might be forgiven.'"

John 1:12–13: "But to all who did receive him, who believed in his name, he gave the right to become children of God, who were born, not of blood nor of the will of the flesh nor of the will of man, but of God."

John 1:29 (GNT): "The next day John saw Jesus coming to him, and said, 'There is the Lamb of God, who takes away the sin of the world!'"

John 3:3: "Jesus answered him, 'Truly, truly, I say to you, unless one is born again he cannot see the kingdom of God.'"

John 3:15–16: "That whoever believes in him may have eternal life. For God so loved the world, that he gave his only Son, that whoever believes in him should not perish but have eternal life."

John 3:18: "Whoever believes in him is not condemned, but whoever does not believe is condemned already, because he has not believed in the name of the only Son of God."

John 6:40: "For this is the will of my Father, that everyone who looks on the Son and believes in him should have eternal life, and I will raise him up on the last day."

John 8:58: "Jesus said to them, 'Truly, truly, I say to you, before Abraham was, I am.'"

John 10:27–30: "My sheep hear my voice, and I know them, and they follow me. I give them eternal life, and they will never perish, and no one will snatch them out of my hand. My Father, who has given them to me, is greater than all, and no one is able to snatch them out of the Father's hand. I and the Father are one."

John 11:25–26: "Jesus said to her, 'I am the resurrection and the life. Whoever believes in me, though he die, yet shall he live, and everyone who lives and believes in me shall never die. Do you believe this?'"

John 12:32: "And I, when I am lifted up from the earth, will draw all people to myself."

John 14:3: "And if I go and prepare a place for you, I will come again and will take you to myself, that where I am you may be also."

John 14:6 "Jesus said to him, 'I am the way, and the truth, and the life. No one comes to the Father except through me.'"

John 15:19: "If you were of the world, the world would love you as its own; but because you are not of the world, but I chose you out of the world, therefore the world hates you."

John 16:27–28: "For the Father himself loves you, because you have loved me and have believed that I came from God. I came from the Father and have come into the world, and now I am leaving the world and going to the Father."

John 17:14: "I have given them your word, and the world has hated them because they are not of the world, just as I am not of the world."

Acts 4:12: "And there is salvation in no one else, for there is no other name under heaven given among men by which we must be saved."

Acts 8:32 (GNT): The passage of scripture which he was reading was this: 'He was like a sheep that is taken to be slaughtered, like a lamb that makes no sound when its wool is cut off. He did not say a word.'"

Romans 3:23–25: "For all have sinned and fall short of the glory of God, and are justified by his grace as a gift, through the redemption that is in Christ Jesus, whom God put forward as a propitiation by his blood, to be received by faith. This was to show God's righteousness, because in his divine forbearance he had passed over former sins."

Romans 4:3–5: "For what does the Scripture say? 'Abraham believed God, and it was counted to him as righteousness.' Now to the one who works, his wages are not counted as a gift but as his due. And to the one who does not work but believes in him who justifies the ungodly, his faith is counted as righteousness."

Romans 5:1–2: "Therefore, since we have been justified by faith, we have peace with God through our Lord Jesus Christ. Through him we have also obtained access by faith into this grace in which we stand, and we rejoice in hope of the glory of God."

Romans 5:8: "But God shows his love for us in that while we were still sinners, Christ died for us."

Romans 5:12: "Therefore, just as sin came into the world through one man, and death through sin, and so death spread to all men because all sinned."

Romans 5:19: "For as by the one man's disobedience the many were made sinners, so by the one man's obedience the many will be made righteous."

Romans 6:23: "For the wages of sin is death, but the free gift of God is eternal life in Christ Jesus our Lord."

Romans 8:1: "There is therefore now no condemnation for those who are in Christ Jesus."

Romans 8:11: "If the Spirit of him who raised Jesus from the dead dwells in you, he who raised Christ Jesus from the dead will also give life to your mortal bodies through his Spirit who dwells in you."

Romans 8:18–22: "For I consider that the sufferings of this present time are not worth comparing with the glory that is to be revealed to us. For the creation waits with eager longing for the revealing of the sons of God. For the creation was subjected to futility, not willingly, but because of him who subjected it, in hope that the creation itself will be set free from its bondage to corruption and obtain the freedom of the glory of the children of God. For we know that the whole creation has been groaning together in the pains of childbirth until now."

Romans 8:39: "Nor height nor depth, nor anything else in all creation, will be able to separate us from the love of God in Christ Jesus our Lord."

Romans 10:9–13: "Because, if you confess with your mouth that Jesus is Lord and believe in your heart that God raised him from the dead, you will be saved. For with the heart one believes and is justified, and with the mouth one confesses and is saved. For the Scripture says, 'Everyone who believes in him will not be put to shame.' For there is no distinction between Jew and Greek; for the same Lord is Lord of all, bestowing his riches on all who call on him. For 'everyone who calls on the name of the Lord will be saved.'"

1 Corinthians 1:18: "For the word of the cross is folly to those who are perishing, but to us who are being saved it is the power of God."

1 Corinthians 15:21–22: "For as by a man came death, by a man has come also the resurrection of the dead. For as in Adam all die, so also in Christ shall all be made alive."

2 Corinthians 5:21 (KJV): "For he hath made him to be sin for us, who knew no sin; that we might be made the righteousness of God in him."

Galatians 3:10–11: "For all who rely on works of the law are under a curse; for it is written, 'Cursed be everyone who does not abide by all things written in the Book of the Law, and do them.' Now it is evident that no one is justified before God by the law, for 'The righteous shall live by faith.'"

Ephesians 2:8–9 (KJV): "For by grace are ye saved through faith; and that not of yourselves: it is the gift of God: Not of works, lest any man should boast."

Philippians 2:9–11: "Therefore God has highly exalted him and bestowed on him the name that is above every name, so that at the name of Jesus every knee should bow, in heaven and on earth and under the earth, and every tongue confess that Jesus Christ is Lord, to the glory of God the Father."

Hebrews 9:27–28 (KJV): "And as it is appointed unto men once to die, but after this the judgment: So Christ was once offered to bear the sins of many; and unto them that look for him shall he appear the second time without sin unto salvation."

God's Word Is the Truth Standard—Not Signs and Wonders

Deuteronomy 8:3: "And he humbled you and let you hunger and fed you with manna, which you did not know, nor did your fathers know, that he might make you know that man does not live by bread alone, but man lives by every word that comes from the mouth of the LORD."

Deuteronomy 13:1–3: "'If a prophet or a dreamer of dreams arises among you and gives you a sign or a wonder, and the sign or wonder that he tells you comes to pass, and if he says, "Let us go after other gods," which you have not known, "and let us serve them," you shall not listen to the words of that prophet or that dreamer of dreams. For the LORD your God is testing you, to know whether you love the LORD your God with all your heart and with all your soul.'"

Psalm 33:4 (KJV): "For the word of the LORD is right; and all his works are done in truth."

Proverbs 1:7: "The fear of the LORD is the beginning of knowledge; fools despise wisdom and instruction."

Ecclesiastes 3:11: "He has made everything beautiful in its time. Also, he has put eternity into man's heart, yet so that he cannot find out what God has done from the beginning to the end."

Matthew 4:4: "But he answered, 'It is written, "Man shall not live by bread alone, but by every word that comes from the mouth of God."'"

Matthew 24:35 (KJV): "Heaven and earth shall pass away, but my words shall not pass away."

Mark 13:22: "For false christs and false prophets will arise and perform signs and wonders, to lead astray, if possible, the elect."

Luke 10:17–18: "The seventy-two returned with joy, saying, 'Lord, even the demons are subject to us in your name!' And he said to them, 'I saw Satan fall like lightning from heaven.'"

Luke 11:28: "But he said, 'Blessed rather are those who hear the word of God and keep it!'"

Luke 21:25–27: "'And there will be signs in sun and moon and stars, and on the earth distress of nations in perplexity because of the roaring of the sea and the waves, people fainting with fear and with foreboding of what is coming on the world. For the powers of the heavens will be shaken. And then they will see the Son of Man coming in a cloud with power and great glory.'"

John 1:14 (KJV): "And the Word was made flesh, and dwelt among us, (and we beheld his glory, the glory as of the only begotten of the Father,) full of grace and truth."

John 17:17 (KJV): "Sanctify them through thy truth: thy word is truth."

Ephesians 1:13 (KJV): "In whom ye also trusted, after that ye heard the word of truth, the gospel of your salvation: in whom also after that ye believed, ye were sealed with that holy Spirit of promise."

Ephesians 6:12: "For we do not wrestle against flesh and blood, but against the rulers, against the authorities, against the cosmic powers over this present darkness, against the spiritual forces of evil in the heavenly places."

Philippians 2:10–11: "So that at the name of Jesus every knee should bow, in heaven and on earth and under the earth, and every tongue confess that Jesus Christ is Lord, to the glory of God the Father."

Colossians 3:16: "Let the word of Christ dwell in you richly, teaching and admonishing one another in all wisdom, singing psalms and hymns and spiritual songs, with thankfulness in your hearts to God."

1 Thessalonians 2:13 (KJV): "For this cause also thank we God without ceasing, because, when ye received the word of God which ye heard of us, ye received it not as the word of men, but as it is in truth, the word of God, which effectually worketh also in you that believe."

1 Timothy 4:1: "Now the Spirit expressly says that in later times some will depart from the faith by devoting themselves to deceitful spirits and teachings of demons."

2 Timothy 3:16 (KJV): "All scripture is given by inspiration of God, and is profitable for doctrine, for reproof, for correction, for instruction in righteousness."

2 Timothy 4:3–4: "For the time is coming when people will not endure sound teaching, but having itching ears they will accumulate for themselves teachers to suit their own passions, and will turn away from listening to the truth and wander off into myths."

Hebrews 4:12: "For the word of God is living and active, sharper than any two-edged sword, piercing to the division of soul and of spirit, of joints and of marrow, and discerning the thoughts and intentions of the heart."

Hebrews 6:5: "And have tasted the goodness of the word of God and the powers of the age to come."

Hebrews 11:3: "By faith we understand that the universe was created by the word of God, so that what is seen was not made out of things that are visible."

James 4:7: "Submit yourselves therefore to God. Resist the devil, and he will flee from you."

1 Peter 1:23: "Since you have been born again, not of perishable seed but of imperishable, through the living and abiding word of God."

2 Peter 1:20–21: "Knowing this first of all, that no prophecy of Scripture comes from someone's own interpretation. For no prophecy was ever produced by the will of man, but men spoke from God as they were carried along by the Holy Spirit."

2 Peter 3:5: "For they deliberately overlook this fact, that the heavens existed long ago, and the earth was formed out of water and through water by the word of God."

1 John 4:4: "Little children, you are from God and have overcome them, for he who is in you is greater than he who is in the world."

Satan Is a Fallen Angel, Liar, and Deceiver with Signs and Wonders

Genesis 3:1: "Now the serpent was more crafty than any other beast of the field that the LORD God had made. He said to the woman, 'Did God actually say, "You shall not eat of any tree in the garden"?'"

Genesis 3:4–5: "But the serpent said to the woman, 'You will not surely die. For God knows that when you eat of it your eyes will be opened, and you will be like God, knowing good and evil.'"

Deuteronomy 13:1–3: "'If a prophet or a dreamer of dreams arises among you and gives you a sign or a wonder, and the sign or wonder that he tells you comes to pass, and if he says, "Let us go after other gods," which you have not known, "and let us serve them," you shall not listen to the words of that prophet or that dreamer of dreams. For the LORD your God is testing you, to know whether you love the LORD your God with all your heart and with all your soul.'"

Isaiah 14:12–15: "'How you are fallen from heaven, O Day Star, son of Dawn! How you are cut down to the ground, you who laid the nations low! You said in your heart, "I will ascend to heaven; above the stars of God I will set my throne on high; I will sit on the mount of assembly in the far reaches of the north; I will ascend above the heights of the clouds; I will make myself like the Most High." But you are brought down to Sheol, to the far reaches of the pit.'"

Jeremiah 10:2: "Thus says the LORD: 'Learn not the way of the nations, nor be dismayed at the signs of the heavens because the nations are dismayed at them.'"

Ezekiel 28:11–17: "Moreover, the word of the LORD came to me: 'Son of man, raise a lamentation over the king of Tyre, and say to him, Thus says the LORD GOD: "You were the signet of perfection, full of wisdom and perfect in beauty. You were in Eden, the garden of God; every precious stone was your covering, sardius, topaz, and diamond, beryl, onyx, and jasper, sapphire, emerald, and carbuncle; and crafted in gold were your settings and your engravings. On the day that you were created they were prepared. You were an anointed guardian cherub. I placed you; you were on the holy mountain of God; in the midst of the stones of fire you walked. You were blameless in your ways from the day you were created, till unrighteousness was found in you. In the abundance of your trade you were filled with violence in your midst, and you sinned; so I cast you as a profane thing from the mountain of God, and I destroyed you, O guardian cherub, from the midst of the stones of fire. Your heart was proud because of your beauty; you corrupted your wisdom for the sake of your splendor. I cast you to the ground; I exposed you before kings, to feast their eyes on you."'"

Matthew 24:24: "For false christs and false prophets will arise and perform great signs and wonders, so as to lead astray, if possible, even the elect."

Matthew 25:41: "Then he will say to those on his left, 'Depart from me, you cursed, into the eternal fire prepared for the devil and his angels.'"

Luke 10:17–18: "The seventy-two returned with joy, saying, 'Lord, even the demons are subject to us in your name!' And he said to them, 'I saw Satan fall like lightning from heaven.'"

Luke 21:11: "There will be great earthquakes, and in various places famines and pestilences. And there will be terrors and great signs from heaven."

John 8:44: "You are of your father the devil, and your will is to do your father's desires. He was a murderer from the beginning, and does not stand in the truth, because there is no truth in him. When he lies, he speaks out of his own character, for he is a liar and the father of lies."

John 12:31: "Now is the judgment of this world; now will the ruler of this world be cast out."

John 14:30: "I will no longer talk much with you, for the ruler of this world is coming. He has no claim on me."

John 16:11: "Concerning judgment, because the ruler of this world is judged."

2 Corinthians 4:3–4: "And even if our gospel is veiled, it is veiled to those who are perishing. In their case the god of this world has blinded the minds of the unbelievers, to keep them from seeing the light of the gospel of the glory of Christ, who is the image of God."

2 Corinthians 11:14–15: "And no wonder, for even Satan disguises himself as an angel of light. So it is no surprise if his servants, also, disguise themselves as servants of righteousness. Their end will correspond to their deeds."

Galatians 1:8: "But even if we or an angel from heaven should preach to you a gospel contrary to the one we preached to you, let him be accursed."

Ephesians 2:1–2: "And you were dead in the trespasses and sins in which you once walked, following the course of this world, following the prince of the power of the air, the spirit that is now at work in the sons of disobedience."

Ephesians 6:12 (KJV): "For we wrestle not against flesh and blood, but against principalities, against powers, against the rulers of the darkness of this world, against spiritual wickedness in high places."

1 Timothy 4:1: "Now the Spirit expressly says that in later times some will depart from the faith by devoting themselves to deceitful spirits and teachings of demons."

2 Timothy 4:3–4: "For the time is coming when people will not endure sound teaching, but having itching ears they will accumulate for themselves teachers to suit their own passions, and will turn away from listening to the truth and wander off into myths."

James 4:7: "Submit yourselves therefore to God. Resist the devil, and he will flee from you."

1 Peter 5:8–9: "Be sober-minded; be watchful. Your adversary the devil prowls around like a roaring lion, seeking someone to devour. Resist him, firm in your faith, knowing that the same kinds of suffering are being experienced by your brotherhood throughout the world."

1 John 4:1: "Beloved, do not believe every spirit, but test the spirits to see whether they are from God, for many false prophets have gone out into the world."

Revelation 12:3–4: "And another sign appeared in heaven: behold, a great red dragon, with seven heads and ten horns, and on his heads seven diadems. His tail swept down a third of the stars of heaven and cast them to the earth. And the dragon stood before the woman who was about to give birth, so that when she bore her child he might devour it."

Revelation 12:7–9: "Now war arose in heaven, Michael and his angels fighting against the dragon. And the dragon and his angels fought back, but he was defeated, and there was no longer any place for them in heaven. And the great dragon was thrown down, that ancient serpent, who is called the devil and Satan, the deceiver of the whole world—he was thrown down to the earth, and his angels were thrown down with him."

Revelation 13:13–14: "It performs great signs, even making fire come down from heaven to earth in front of people, and by the signs that it is allowed to work in the presence of the beast it deceives those who dwell on earth, telling them to make an image for the beast that was wounded by the sword and yet lived."

Revelation 16:14–16: "For they are demonic spirits, performing signs, who go abroad to the kings of the whole world, to assemble them for battle on the great day of God the Almighty. ('Behold, I am coming like a thief! Blessed is the one who stays awake, keeping his garments on, that he may not go about naked and be seen exposed!') And they assembled them at the place that in Hebrew is called Armageddon."

Revelation 19:20: "And the beast was captured, and with it the false prophet who in its presence had done the signs by which he deceived those who had received the mark of the beast and those who worshiped its image. These two were thrown alive into the lake of fire that burns with sulfur."

Revelation 20:2–3: "And he seized the dragon, that ancient serpent, who is the devil and Satan, and bound him for a thousand years, and threw him into the pit, and shut it and sealed it over him, so that he might not deceive the nations any longer, until the thousand years were ended. After that he must be released for a little while."

Revelation 20:7–10: "And when the thousand years are ended, Satan will be released from his prison and will come out to deceive the nations that are at the four corners of the earth, Gog and Magog, to gather them for battle; their number is like the sand of the sea. And they marched up over the broad plain of the earth and surrounded the camp of the saints and the beloved city, but fire came down from heaven and consumed them, and the devil who had deceived them was thrown into the lake of fire and sulfur where the beast and the false prophet were, and they will be tormented day and night forever and ever."

Endnotes

1 https://www.cbsnews.com/news/alien-intelligent-life-other-planets/.

2 Gary Bates (2010): *Alien Intrusion: UFOs and the Evolution Connection*, Master Books, ISBN: 0-89051, Library of Congress Number 2004118184.

3 Chuck Missler and Mark Eastman (1997): *Alien Encounters: The Secret Behind the UFO Phenomenon*, Koinonia House.

4 John Mack M.D. (1994): *Abduction: Human Encounters with Aliens*, Charles Scribner's Sons, New York.

5 James T. Lacatski, D. Eng., Colm A. Kelleher, Ph.D., and George Knapp (2021): *Skinwalkers at the Pentagon: An Insiders Account of the Secret Government UFO Program*, RTMA, LLC, Henderson, Nevada.

6 Richard Strothers: https:pubs.giss.nasa.gov/docs/2007/2007_strothers_st02710y.pdf.

7 For anyone interested in investigating NDEs, I recommend the book *Imagine Heaven* by John Burke.

8 www.newsweek.com/43-americans-are-more-interested-aliens-after-pertagon-ufo-report-1598804.

ORDER INFORMATION

To order additional copies of this book, please visit
www.redemption-press.com.
Also available at Christian bookstores and Barnes and Noble.

CPSIA information can be obtained
at www.ICGtesting.com
Printed in the USA
LVHW042122040623
748855LV00004B/602

9 781646 456864